essence

essence

THE MANIFESTO OF JESUS

Roger Ellis

scm

Endorsements

"Within five minutes of picking up this book you will realise that Roger Ellis is a man who has made Christ's manifesto his own. It pulses with passion and contagious excitement and conceals theology within simple, accessible language. *Essence* conveys hard-won lessons from half a lifetime of leading, pastoring, preaching and pioneering. It applies God's living Word to the modern world. It is the theology of parable and praxis, illustrated with testimony and overflowing in prayer.

"This is a book about 'revelation': Revelation, the church that Roger planted; the revelation of Jesus Christ in the Word of God; and the revelations of a seasoned and much-loved leader in the body of Christ."

Pete Greig – 24-7 Prayer and Alpha International

"In *Essence*, Roger Ellis shows us both the heart and the breadth of Christian life and faith. The heart is the person of Jesus and the breadth is his continuing ministry, spelt out in Nazareth and still impacting every aspect of life. Best of all are the stories of messy lives being transformed. A book for anyone who wants to be a disciple without getting too religious."

Graham Cray – Archbishops' Missioner

scm

First published in Great Britain by Son Christian Media in 2011

Son Christian Media
PO Box 3070
Littlehampton
West Sussex
BN17 6WX

British Library Cataloguing in Publication Data
A record of this book is available from the British Library

ISBN: 978-0-9569464-0-9

Design and typesetting by Andy Ashdown Design
www.andyashdowndesign.co.uk

Manufactured in Great Britain by Halcyon

To Chloe and James:

Fire for your heart and light for your journey.

Contents

Foreword

If you've never met Roger Ellis, now is your chance – he is all over his own book. "Well", you say, "that is not surprising – it is *his* book!" However, not every author's energy pours through every line. His excitement, his haste, his words of wisdom – which hardly have time to finish their sentences – his half-enunciated statements and embryonic ideas, his compassions and cryptic stories cut down to the fewest words since he must get them out, all bring to us the passionate, tender-hearted disciple of Jesus who wants us to join him in his never-ending discovery of God and His ways.

Roger wants us to continue on in our faith in the same way as he has, as a journey of discovery. We will walk together through the book, questioning and challenging the well-worn truths to find new angles and nuances of revelation. Sometimes we will want to agree and at other times not. These points of discovery, agreements or otherwise in our walking together are less important than our common willingness and commitment to see more of Jesus.

Roger has a favourite biblical text, or *passage* as he calls it, from the prophet Isaiah. Isaiah 61:1 onwards is used to define the pathway we will take through the five chapters of his book.

These beautiful verses, loved and used by the Lord Jesus Christ, will keep us on track, defining our parameters of research and inquiry. Roger has a good precedent for this approach; Jesus himself preached on this, explaining the prophecy and how he fulfilled it. I wonder how the lead up to this event unfolded in Jesus' life? Perhaps it happened like this:

It seemed to be a normal Saturday morning. No work today, time for the family meal together and a short outing walking to the meeting place. However, on this particular weekend as we approached the assembly rooms there appeared to be a buzz of excited chattering.

"One of our boys has come back to his home town. You know, Joseph the carpenter's son. He left his trade here in Nazareth a few weeks ago to take up preaching. Not much money in that, we all said, but here he is back home having made at least a bit of a reputation and has even produced a few healings so they say."

Everyone pressed into the local synagogue; it seemed a bit small this Saturday. We were all hoping the minister would give the scroll of Scripture to Joseph's boy Jesus. We, his own townsfolk, should have had the first chance to test him out.

"Surely he will preach today?!"

"I hope so, but you know what some of those oldies are like, they think they know it all and Jesus is only just passed thirty – what can he know that's new?"

"Oh, look, he is standing up and they've given him the Scriptures. He is going to read – what's the reading today, Isaiah 61?"

> *"The Spirit of the Lord God is upon me,*
> *because the Lord has anointed me*

to bring good news to the afflicted;
He has sent me to bind up the brokenhearted,
to proclaim liberty to captives
and freedom to prisoners;
To proclaim the favourable year of the Lord
and the day of vengeance of our God;
To comfort all who mourn,
to grant those who mourn in Zion,
giving them a garland instead of ashes,
the oil of gladness instead of mourning,
the mantle of praise instead of a spirit of fainting
so they will be called oaks of righteousness,
the planting of the Lord, that he may be glorified" (Isaiah 61:1-3).

Jesus closed the book, gave it back to the attendant and sat down. The atmosphere was electric – every eye was fixed on Jesus. We had heard these words many times before, we could recite them perfectly like any pop song lyrics, but today it was different. As Jesus read them they appeared to fit in a way we had never known; like a glove slipping over a hand. The Spirit of the Lord God was indeed on him to preach, to proclaim, to heal, enlighten, and bring good news with grace and favour. These words seemed to be made for Jesus. "He's one of ours you know – I was at synagogue school with his brother and know his sisters as well."

He should have known better, though. We would have followed him to the ends of the earth but he shouldn't have spoiled it all. We were eating out of the palm of his hand and he goes and talks about God blessing and healing in the Bible just as he was doing, but not to our lot – to other races! It made the oldies indignant and furious and we soon caught the spirit. I don't know what got into us, but we were just about to murder him, would you believe it! Of course, we knew he was wrong and so did the elders. We couldn't put up with that. We've read the good news so many times, we know what it says. There isn't really anything new; we were mistaken to think that it fitted Jesus so well, and that he filled it out in a fresh way.

Many, like these of Jesus' day, think they know all there is to know about Christ and Christianity. Roger would not claim that he knows more than everyone else, he simply invites us to investigate with him afresh; to look for fuller meaning, to fill out the glove of Scripture as it is filled with Jesus' living hand. Knowing we all need God's mercy as we journey together as children who are willing to learn. Jesus promises that such are candidates for truth: "I thank you, Father… that you have hidden these things from the wise and clever and have revealed them to babes" (Matthew 11:25), for such may enter the kingdom of heaven.

Reading Roger's book will be a journey, not to find every answer and put other people straight, but to experience more of Jesus and his active reign in our lives.

Roger Forster
London, March 2011

INTRODUCTION

The Bible is the 'book of books' in more ways than one. To those with ears to hear and eyes to see it provides revelatory insight into the heart and mind of God and lays out the big story of 'all that is', from inception to eternity. In broad terms, it addresses the issue of where we have come from and moreover presents a vision of where we are going.

This story spans thousands of years and moves across different cultures and time zones. It is presented by different authors in different books, each reflecting their unique cultural lens, experience and writing style. Some wrote history, others poetry, some told stories while others wrote in apocalyptic riddles. While there is much diversity, each plays a unique part in revealing the plans and purposes of God, leading us to the place where we can know both what he is like and also experience the reality of a relationship with him.

The Bible's testimony about itself is that it is "breathed out by God" (2 Timothy 3:16). Although Scripture bears the imprint of the eyes, ears, mouths and hearts of the authors, God ensured that his pure flow of inspiration runs through this vast river of material. This sets its course and maintains its purity, quality and 'DNA' as it runs over and around the rocky and varied terrain of human culture, history and relationships. It also seeps underground through the porous bedrock of human nature, sinfulness and imperfection; washing out all kinds of precious deposits, detritus and debris.

As a result, it is both invaluable and uniquely authoritative, while at the same time being occasionally quirky, difficult and hard to grasp. Its value is not just as a shaper of worldview and a guidebook for life, but as a living model of what happens when God's will begins to break into the earth and land in the lives of different people, with different experiences.

These include the good, the bad and the ugly; the poor and the rich; the oppressed and even the dictators. Cultures infected by decadence and others striving for goodness. It reaches to people who are far away from God, the lost, the ordinary, refugees and kings, adulterers, murderers, lovers, warriors and God-seekers. When God's kingdom comes to earth and interacts with people like us it's messy, volatile and complicated. It's also challenging and exciting because, within the narrative of Scripture, treasures are waiting to be discovered, and these can lead to the fulfilment of all our deepest longings. This fulfilment lies in the knowledge and experience of the love of God.

As a result, we can't do without the Bible, and if we neglect it we will ultimately lose our edge and wander off course. No matter how inspired by the Holy Spirit we may feel, or how safe or 'right' we stand within our own tradition, without the continued tutelage and shaping of Scripture we are at the mercy of our own opinions, imperfections and preferences. It's a recipe for disaster!

My father-in-law was a young Jewish boy in a public school in England just after the Second World War. Anti-Semitism was not unique to Germany and he was bullied, persecuted and assaulted verbally, right from the outset. The central space for this persecution was around the meal table at school.

One day he came across a Bible in the school library and began to read it like a novel. He read the whole book several times and began to realise that the hero of the Bible was Jesus Christ, and that the whole story was built around him. Furthermore, he came to suspect that this book told more than a story. Its hero was raised from the dead, was alive and appeared to answer prayers. He wondered whether it might be true and real. That night he prayed a simple prayer to God. "God if you are real, please stop their words." He awoke the next day wondering what would happen.

To his absolute astonishment, not only did the cruel words stop, every word stopped – it was as if he were invisible! Despite being around people throughout the whole day, not a single person either spoke to him or acknowledged his existence. He was astonished!

This remarkable experience was enough to set him on a journey of discovery, which became more concrete when he met Christians at university, who explained to him what relationship with God through Jesus Christ is all about.

This is a great story, which shows us many things. The chief things it tells us is obvious, even to a young Jewish boy who had never encountered the Bible: that Jesus Christ is the central figure to the whole narrative. Everything before Jesus chronologically points to him and everything post-Jesus flows from him. He is the "Alpha and Omega" (Revelation 1:8), the beginning and the end, the "cornerstone" (Isaiah 28:16; Zechariah 10:4; Ephesians 2:20; 1Peter 2:6). He holds everything together, he's the Messiah, the Son of God, the Son of Man, the "Word made flesh - God in a body revealed to us" (John 1:14). In him lies the fulfilment of all hope and longing. In the words of Jesus: "If you have seen me you have seen the Father" (John 14:9).

This centrality of Jesus Christ to the whole story of God has led to an approach to the Bible that can be observed throughout the history of the Church and is sometimes called the 'Christocentric Hermeneutic'.

In essence, this means that Jesus is the highest possible fulfilment of God's purposes and our "Immanuel" (Isaiah 7:14), which means "God with us, revealed to us." So he should also be the lens through which we look at Scripture and begin to answer the questions we may have about the Bible or God.

He is the interpretive key and, if we keep him as our focus, we can't go far wrong.

Furthermore, any questions around life, morality, truth, relationships and lifestyle should be looked at through the portal of Jesus' life and teaching, even if the core texts addressing the issue are found elsewhere in the Bible.

Sadly, throughout church history, Christians have struggled to keep this clear focus. As a result, 'religion' often appears distant from the essence of the message Jesus Christ came to proclaim and from the example he set. When this happens Christianity loses its way. Faith becomes absorbed by tradition, service, institution and lust for power. As a result the core message of Jesus is lost, as are many of the people he came to find and save.

In many cases, the loss of the lens of Jesus means that we have a legalistic fundamentalism that is biblically non-Christian! It uses Scripture to support its conclusions, but in heart, content and application it is a million miles away from the 'Spirit of Christ'.

The passage below addresses this problem. It could be said that there is no other place in the Bible that so clearly defines the heart, passion and purposes of Jesus Christ. It's a passage that has been claimed by people on opposite sides of many arguments: by evangelists, activists, liberationists, healers and politicians alike. It's applied personally, corporately, individually, socially, internally, externally, literally, metaphorically, practically and supernaturally.

It's read with many different lenses by different streams of thought and each is convinced of its core importance.

I believe it's vital for us today to have a fresh encounter with these verses and to allow them to envision and inform in a vital way.

We need a Jesus movement more than anything else.

Luke 4:16-21 says:

> *And he stood up to read. The scroll of the prophet Isaiah was handed to him. Unrolling it, he found the place where it is written:*
>
> *"The Spirit of the Lord is on me, because he has anointed me to preach good news to the poor.*

He has sent me to proclaim freedom for the prisoners
and recovery of sight for the blind,
to release the oppressed, to proclaim the year of the Lord's favour."

Then he rolled up the scroll, gave it back to the attendant and sat down. The eyes of everyone in the synagogue were fastened on him, and he began by saying to them, "Today, this scripture is fulfilled in your hearing."

These verses are vitally important. They have been referred to by many commentators as the 'manifesto' of Jesus. For some this creates a problem, as we live in an age when many of us have been totally disillusioned by politics and politicians. The moment the word 'manifesto' is mentioned, we begin to glaze over.

Our default setting is to be suspicious and cynical, lacking in faith and hope. However, here we are encountering Jesus, the Messiah, the Son of God, and he is unpacking the whole rationale for his life, death and resurrection. He is laying out his manifesto; what he will live for, die for; his core 'raison d'être'.

These words are truly radical and portray the core passions and intentions of God. This passage is absolutely core and unique. One meaning of the word "radical" is "coming back to our roots". These verses take us back to our roots as believers in Christ and show us the colour that all Christians should bleed. It shows us what should be on our hearts, filling our prayers, booked in our diaries, consuming our energies and spending our resources.

It should cause us to ask some difficult questions. What are the things that we should be really passionate about? What are the things within our world and in the lives of people that should get us fired up? What are our visions and dreams? Where should our visions and dreams fit within the sphere of God's purposes? All of these things can be found within this passage.

In verse 18, Jesus talks about "preaching". This word is very interesting. It's so much richer than someone waxing eloquently or issuing pious platitudes. It's the Greek word "kerygma", which literally means "the essential formula", the "essence".

So what Jesus is revealing here is the very core of who he is and the very essence of the good news he is giving to humanity to experience, live, communicate and outwork in the whole of creation. In short, it's totally and utterly essential!

In the New Testament Church, the word "kerygma" came to summarise the apostolic preaching of the gospel in Acts. The early church was very focused. There was a core teaching, a core lifestyle; they were very 'centred'.

Today, Christians can be anything but focused on the core. Tossed to and fro by theological controversies and cultural agendas, we often lose sight of what it's all about.

All too often our 'centre' is either around the maintenance of tradition, a consumer approach to spirituality, or the creation of a 'post-modern faith niche', which at times gains more energy and impetus by asserting what it's not than it does by the creation of fresh life and innovative expressions of this 'essential core', which is what really matters.

We need refreshing and, as we look at the New Testament Church, seeing them so centred around the person of Jesus and the message of Jesus, we are refocused and re-energised.

Today many Christians are looking for the way forward. Some are looking for supernatural experiences, others for justice, many for community, others for more authentic expressions of Church, while others feel lost and disconnected.

I'm suggesting that whatever we are looking for, this is the place to start.

I was dismayed to read in *Time* magazine that, at the time of writing, Neo-Calvinism was one of the top five ideas in America. My first thought was: 'How sad is that?!' This is not a reflection on Calvinism, Neo-Calvinism, Arminianism, Neo-Arminianism or any other 'ism'!

Perhaps, at best, this trend is a reflection of the desire within the Church to find keys to the future in the past, and at worst a manifestation of human agendas and divisions, which contribute very little positively to the cause of Jesus Christ. I found this so sad because the focus of the Bible is not Calvinism but Jesus! We are not called to follow 'isms' or human theological constructs but Jesus Christ.

This passage cries out for us to embrace a bit of 'Neo-Jesus', 'Neo New Testament Christianity'. We shouldn't, in my opinion, desire to recreate the very things in church history (for example divides around Calvinism and Arminianism) that have arguably produced questionable fruit in the past.

Rather, we should desire to connect with who Christ Jesus is, his core values and his message to humanity. This will light our fires and plot our course towards an expression of faith that is undeniably authentic, real and transformational. This will create for us the hermeneutic we need, which is centred in Jesus

Christ and able to connect with people in whatever context we find ourselves.

This message will take us way out of our comfort zones and engage us at different levels. It will engage minds and hearts. It will challenge our strategies and cause us to be focused on people and humanity, while at the same time looking at the bigger picture around us.

Rather than taking it verse by verse, I will be examining five main themes that run through the passage. These are: Source, Good News, People, Big Picture and Economy.

CHAPTER 1:

SOURCE

When Jesus stands up to read at the synagogue there are no clues as to how the text was chosen. Has he arrived on time, providentially and prophetically to read the passage that was due to be read at that time and place? Did he choose the reading or was the reading chosen for him? Commentators offer different opinions on this.

One thing is for sure. Right at the beginning of the passage, in verse 17, Jesus declares:

"The Spirit of the Lord is on me..."

In verse 21, he says:

"Today this Scripture is fulfilled in your hearing."

The passage Jesus reads is from Isaiah 61:1-2 and is about the mission and identity of the Messiah. Jesus is basically saying: "I am the complete fulfilment of the Old Testament dream of a Messiah. I am the one that you are looking for."

Jesus had been on the earth for thirty years and, although Scripture records some facts about his life on earth to date, this is where the plot begins to accelerate. This is the first time he's spoken publicly and he's choosing his words very, very carefully.

The Jews met in the synagogue, not having a temple or the ability to offer their own sacrifices. They would meet week by week for the reading of Scripture, preaching and worship. Jesus was invited in and, whether he was randomly offered the passage or he chose it, he stood up to read.

This is what some would call a "kairos" moment, a "now" moment. A time when the world is changed and culture is shifted; a moment that changes history.

It's a moment that captured the attention of the world, shook the world order and launched a myriad of conspiracy theories. It's like the release of Nelson Mandela or the breaking down of the Berlin Wall. It's a moment of breakthrough, like man's first walk on the moon.

The importance of some of these moments is not always grasped at the time they occur. On other occasions their significance dims in the eyes of many during subsequent decades. In the 1980s, people tired of the idea of moon landings and so NASA incredibly taped over some of the original film of the event! Precious and unique footage lost forever because of the price of a tape and the effort of storage.

It's my belief that we have lost the impact and import of this biblical treasure, and one of the keys to the flourishing of faith in any aeon is the rediscovery of the mission and mandate of Jesus Christ by a Church that has the passion and energy to do something about it.

This is a historical moment. None of us are the Messiah (and if we think we are we are in need of therapy!). But most of us will experience "kairos" moments at key times in our lives. Times when our history is changed forever, when we decide to adopt faith, move to a new location, choose a vocation (or a vocation chooses us) or when we face bereavements, marriage or the birth of a child.

I believe this passage offers the opportunity of kairos moments to all who would embrace them as we engage with it and we realise that the Spirit of the Lord can be upon us. With this reality and experience come the resources to outwork the calling of Jesus Christ in today's world, making his calling our calling.

This passage can unlock very significant moments. It summons us to be ready to see the fulfilment of God's will in our lives and opens a window of opportunity through which we can see into the heart of the kingdom that comes in part as we pray, "Your kingdom come". This kingdom will come in fullness at the end of the age.

Context

As Jesus declares the fulfilment of this Scripture he's referring to the prophet Isaiah. As we look through the book of Isaiah we realise that so much of it is about the coming Messiah. I have no space to examine much of the material here but there are some key passages that warrant our attention now and we shall look at others in subsequent chapters.

In Isaiah 9:2-7 we have a passage that's often the centre of the Christian celebration of Christmas. It's such a shame that for many this is the only time we focus on the incarnation, since it's such a key moment for the whole of history.

Verse two declares: *"The people in darkness have seen a great light; on those living in the land of the shadow of death a light has dawned."*

Verse six continues: *"For to us a child is born, to us a son is given, and the government will be on his shoulders. And he will be called Wonderful Counsellor, Mighty God, Everlasting Father, Prince of Peace."*

Right at the heart of the prophetic message concerning the Messiah is this sense of incarnation, God becoming man, and his kingdom – God's reign and rule –breaking into the earth.

These are, without doubt, two mega themes for the Church and encapsulate the whole purpose of God in this age.

Jesus came as fully God and fully human, touching the whole of creation through his incarnation, life, death, resurrection and ascension. God's chosen method of redemption involved his coming to earth and fully identifying with us, 'fleshing out' his love and purposes. As followers of Jesus we are called to incarnate the message of the Christ. Our proclamation is not intended to be disembodied but clothed with our lifestyle. Through our love, our heart, our community and through our relationships, we are called to incarnate, to flesh out, the love of Jesus.

This is what the gospel of Jesus Christ is all about. It's what mission is all about and it's also what God's kingdom is about; God's life, presence, values and agenda breaking in now. It's about heaven coming to earth. God's reign and rule, God's healing, God's goodness, God's forgiveness and God's justice - and many other things beside.

This is the hope that is held out by the manifesto of Jesus and is offered for us to experience now. We taste heaven as a deposit of the future; a glimpse of the fullness of God's glory that will one day come to earth.

So right from his birth Jesus began to fulfil Isaiah 9. I would recommend you take time to read Isaiah chapter 40 through to the end of 61, it's absolutely amazing.

So much of Isaiah's prophetic ministry speaks first to his current context and then beyond this to the future hope. We will come across many of these passages as we look at Luke 4:17-21, which is based on a reading from Isaiah 61:1-2, which in turn draws and builds on so much of the 'messianic material' earlier in the book.

When I first met my now wife Maggie she was a fresh-faced 16-year-old and had just spent part of her holidays doing street evangelism on the subway within New York's Jewish community. She was working with an organisation called Jews for Jesus, whose evangelistic approach at that time was very upfront. The Orthodox Jews are all too aware of the potential application of many of their messianic scriptures to Jesus. One of the T-shirts she wore carried the words "Jesus made me kosher", but the one that caused by far the most intense reaction read merely "Isaiah 53". As she stood wearing the T-shirt, without speaking, she was sworn at, spat on and questioned in depth.

Isaiah 53:1-6 reads:

Who has believed our message
and to whom has the arm of the Lord been revealed?
He grew up before him like a tender shoot, and like a root out of dry ground.

He had no beauty or majesty to attract us to him,
nothing in his appearance that we should desire him.
He was despised and rejected by men, a man of sorrows, and familiar with suffering.
Like one from whom men hide their faces he was despised and we esteemed him not.
Surely he took up our infirmities and carried our sorrows,
yet we considered him stricken by God,
smitten by him, and afflicted.
But he was pierced for our transgressions,
he was crushed for our iniquities;
the punishment that brought us peace was upon him,
and by his wounds we are healed.
We all like sheep, have gone astray each of us has turned to his own way; and the Lord has laid on him the iniquity of us all.

When put in the context of the whole chapter and viewed in the light of the eventual death of Jesus on the cross, we see how much the destiny of Jesus and the identity of Jesus as Messiah is foretold by the prophet. It is truly remarkable.

Jesus also saw himself in this way and makes a clear reference to Isaiah 53:12 as he draws near to his crucifixion, as we see in Luke 22:37:

"It is written: 'And he was numbered with the transgressors', and I tell you that this must be fulfilled in me. Yes, what is written about me is reaching its fulfilment."

And so we move to Isaiah 61:1-2:

The Spirit of the sovereign Lord is on me, because the Lord has anointed me to preach good news to the poor.

He has sent me to bind up the broken-hearted,
to proclaim freedom for the captives,
and release from darkness for the prisoners.

This leads us to begin to appreciate the drama and effect when, at the end of his reading, Jesus announces: "I am the fulfilment of all of these things."

Empowered

Jesus proclaims: "The Spirit of the sovereign Lord is upon me." As we shall see, the Holy Spirit is ever-present in the life of Jesus; right from his miraculous conception through to his ascension to be at the right hand of the Father when he released the Holy Spirit to come upon his followers and all those who would follow in their footsteps (Acts 1:5, 1 Corinthians 12:7-11, 28).

In the creation narrative, we see the Holy Spirit hovering over the as-yet unformed earth (Genesis 1:1-2). We see the Word being spoken by God and in John 1:1 we see that Jesus is that Word.

In creation we see God at work, and the jigsaw pieces of the nature of God and his plans are progressively put together through every book of the Bible from Genesis to Revelation. As we then look in retrospect we see that right from the beginning of creation, God (in the form of the Trinity) was central to proceedings, with the Holy Spirit acting as a key creative and empowering agent throughout the whole process.

In Luke 1:35 we see that the Holy Spirit is involved integrally in the conception of Jesus as the Spirit of the Lord overcomes, overshadows, or comes upon Mary. The same Spirit that hovered over the waters and was active in creation was also involved in the miraculous impregnation of Mary so Jesus could be fully human and fully God. Fully God in his miraculous conception yet descended from David both in human lineage and also sharing in the same anointing and empowering from the heavenly Father.

By being called the "Christ", Jesus is being shown as not just 'an' anointed (empowered) one but 'the' anointed one, "Christ" being the Greek word for "Messiah".

The title Messiah occurs for the first time in a predictive sense in Daniel 9:25-6, which predicts that an anointed one will come and complete God's purposes. In this text the idea of fulfilment and completion are paramount.

The absorption of the person and activity of Jesus in the work and activity of the Spirit of the Lord continues as his life and ministry take shape.

The Holy Spirit descends on Jesus at his baptism in Luke 3:21-22. Now what a baptism that is! Most of us are content with a short testimony and some prayers and promises, Jesus has the Holy Spirit of God descending upon him like a dove and an audible voice from heaven bringing God's approval, saying: "This is my Son, with whom I am well pleased."

In Luke 4, Jesus is led into the desert by the Holy Spirit and is tempted by the devil. It's noteworthy here that the Holy Spirit doesn't always lead us into the easiest of situations. This was the beginning of Jesus' exposure and the difficult journey that was to culminate in his purposed death and resurrection.

How did he sustain himself, how did he perform his miracles, how did he manage to be tempted in every way just as we are, yet without giving in to sin (Hebrews 4:15)?

It's clear from the New Testament that when he was on the earth, Jesus operated in the same way that you and I need to; that is, under the strengthening and anointing of the Holy Spirit. Although he was "fully God", there is a sense in which he also took on the vulnerable "nature of a servant", sharing our human weaknesses and frailty (Philippians 2: 6-11).

In this act, Jesus laid aside the option of operating 'Bruce Almighty style' regarding the miraculous. He learned to respond to the voice of the Father and lived in humble dependence upon him. He received the Spirit of the Lord in his humanity and operated in the Spirit's power in exactly the same way that you or I might now operate. Jesus has pioneered our path.

Jesus goes as the ultimate marked man, as a servant and with human frailty into the presence of evil in its fullest expression. He emerged triumphant because he stayed close to the presence of God and remained ruthless in obedience to the Father. He took no shortcuts and was ready to embrace his destiny.

In Luke 4:14 we see Jesus returning in the power of the Spirit and then things really start to move quickly.

Within the life of Jesus we see the preparation and ongoing work of the Holy Spirit. The Spirit broods over him, leads him, develops him and empowers him.

Do you want to walk this way with God? Maybe you have already had a go at it. This passage challenges us to go the whole way. Jesus operated under the power of the Holy Spirit: how much more do we require the presence of God to make sense of our lives, equip us to serve God and to achieve anything meaningful?

The same Spirit that filled the life of Jesus wants to fill our lives. Jesus showed us the way.

My prayer coming out of this is:

> *Lord, just as your Spirit hovers over my life, I want to yield to you. I want you to lead me and take me and bring me to the place that you want me to be. I want you to bend me, I want you to break me, so that I can be used by you. I want to be an agent of your message, of your kingdom. I want to experience everything you have for my life. Come fill me with your Spirit and keep filling me day by day as I appear to leak!*

Both Luke 4:18 and Isaiah 61:1 declare that the Spirit of the Lord is upon Jesus.

The meaning of the word Messiah carries a sense of crowning, appointing and setting apart; an accrediting, equipping and investing of favour.

In the Old Testament the idea of anointing certain people for specific tasks was common. The anointing with oil symbolised the setting apart of a person for a specific task with the appropriate authorisation for it. Priests, kings and prophets were all anointed.

As Christopher Wright observes:

"The anointed person was set aside and equipped by God and for God, so that what he or she did was in God's name, with the help of God's Spirit, under God's protection and with God's authority."

This is what happened to Jesus and it's also what happens to us when we respond to God's call. The presence of Jesus comes upon us through the Holy Spirit.

The word Christ means literally "covered with oil". Oil is often a biblical symbol for the Holy Spirit. I believe all of us should aspire to be drenched, to be covered with the oil of the Holy Spirit in everything we do.

As we're going to see in later chapters, a key to the whole process of seeing the prayer we are called to pray, "Your kingdom come, your will be done, on earth as it is in heaven", is the Holy Spirit. This is the prayer that we're called to pray and the life we're called to live, and to do this we need to be equipped, just as Jesus was.

This is one of the most important keys to seeing God's reign and rule breaking out in our families, marriages, lives, communities, schools, businesses and churches. Believe it or not, the Holy Spirit is key. Being filled with the Holy Spirit opens the door for God to move in us and through us in ways we could not have previously imagined. It doesn't matter where you are, how gifted you are, how independent you are or how unworthy you feel, this is what we all need.

My wife Maggie runs a charity called Lifecentre, which is a counselling service for people who have been raped and sexually abused: men and women, old and young, from all backgrounds. Members of the team work professionally and counsel Christians, but most of the people they counsel are not Christians.

It is funded by statutory bodies, all of its counsellors are trained and the whole organisation is very professional. It has gifted, talented and well qualified people giving of themselves at every level of the charity. This is a minimum requirement as the team is working with the vulnerable as well as with many statutory bodies. Lifecentre has grown considerably in recent years.

But what's the key? Is the key professionalism? Is the key my wife's giftedness? Is it that she's a focused person? Certainly this all helps. She is so focused on justice and healing for those broken by sexual violence that attempting to divert her would be rather like attempting to rugby tackle a herd of stampeding hippopotamuses. Not that she looks like a hippo, but when she's in full flight there's only one way you're going to bring her down! I don't try it that often, it's not worth my while.

Is the success of Lifecentre merely to do with this vibrant and sacrificial compassion? To look at it the other way, where do these remarkable qualities come from? From where does the remarkable commitment, resilience and competence of the many Lifecentre volunteers emanate?

We know more than anybody that it's to do with the Holy Spirit. Right at the beginning, when the burden and the desire to work among the sexually abused and broken had barely emerged, Dale Gentry, a speaker from the US with a reputation for prophetic ministry, arrived at our church unaware of the vision that had already begun to roughly form. Before a single piece of work was done he spoke these words:

> *The Holy Spirit says you are going to have a life centre, where you restore people back to life. You will have young ladies and young men whose lives are dark, on the verge of committing suicide, [who have] gone through several abortions, been raped many times, abused by their fathers and mothers, [who have] no*

life. There is going to be a life centre here, L.I.F.E., a LIFE centre. You will take people and nurse them back to life. For whom much is forgiven, much will be required.

Whom you nurse back God says much will be required. I will restore them sevenfold and they will be mighty; mighty warriors. So God says I am going to give you a life centre where people get their lives back. They will come broken and confused, misused and mistreated; you will nurse them back to life. Pour on the wine and the oil, send them out to do mighty things.

This is the day, says the Lord, that I will turn the hearts of the fathers back to the children, and I am turning the hearts of the children back to the Father, putting families back together at the life centre. It will be a place like no other place. It'll be a place where people get their lives back; it'll be a place where people get their families back. It will be a place where people get rid of their shame.

It'll be a place where **Isaiah 61** *will come to pass - "in the place of your shame I will give you double honour". They get their life back, they get their childhood back, they get their youth back, they get their families back, they get their reputations back, they get their self-worth back at the life centre.*

I see young people being wheeled in here on stretchers because they have no life left in them; they don't even want to get out of bed. They are actually brought here on stretchers because they say "I am not going to get up". They come to the life centre and they get their lives back. They get their reputations back. They get their purity back, they get their virginity back. They are wheeled in here but they walk out, they run out, hop out, jump out, skip out.

> *I see entire families moving here because they are so broken and their children are so bewildered and their last resort is to come here and become a part of the life centre. It's bigger than you think it is. It's not a little place in the corner; it's a mega place...*

This was an incredible moment, a 'kairos moment', and knowing what I know about how things have developed I still cannot read these words without tears.

This prophetic word is on the wall at the Lifecentre offices. Senior officers in the police force have visited and have been observed musing over it because many have said that there's something different about Lifecentre. At one fundraising event a distinguished speaker was unable to give her presentation as she was overwhelmed, not by the issues, but by the sense that something (or someone, in actual fact) really special was present.

Many have commented that there's a unique peace at the Lifecentre, and all the Christians there know, without doubt, where that comes from.

What is it that makes us distinctive as Christians? What is it that sets us apart? It's only that the Lord is with us. It's precious little to do with us, as even our best efforts and obedience are energised by God's Spirit and made possible by his grace and provision.

What made Jesus so full of life and zeal? It's that he was anointed by the Holy Spirit. This is the root of true zeal and passion. So if you would like to know what the anointing of the Holy Spirit is all about, ask him to come; let the Holy Spirit fill you.

If you want to know what the anointing of the Spirit is like, and what the Holy Spirit will most likely begin to do in and through you, then read on in Luke 4. He's into good news for the poor, freedom for the prisoners, recovery of sight for the blind, release for the oppressed and bestowing of the Lord's favour!

An era

Isaiah 61:2 and Luke 4:19 introduce the whole idea of the "year of the Lord's favour". Jesus brings us the idea that in him God has inaugurated a new era. An era is a period of time marked by a distinctive character. And the whole time between Jesus' first coming, which we're reading about here, and the return of Christ, which is yet to occur, is the era of salvation. We are caught up in this era, which is characterised by the message of the "servant", another name given to the Messiah by Isaiah in his book. Throughout this time, the experience of followers of Jesus Christ will be that "the Spirit of the Lord is upon us".

The challenge to us here is: will we allow the era of our lives to be absorbed in the era of salvation?

I don't know how many of you have studied past revival movements within Christianity. There have been Methodist, Salvationist and Pentecostal, revivals, among others.

You look at some of the pictures of these old saints. They look a bit crusty, but the truth is they just had different fashion sense in those days!

You then look more closely into their eyes and at their achievements and begin to reflect on the hundreds of years and thousands upon thousands of men and women and churches that have gone before us and have done amazing things.

They've come and gone and their movements have often diminished, yet they have left us with an amazing legacy. There are stories of people who have lived and died; some have even been raised from the dead. Many were saved from the gutter, others from the highest echelons of society.

Our forebears have lived for God and transformed nations. They have fed the poor, changed legal systems and covered the globe with the light of the good news of Jesus.

The Spirit of the Lord was surely upon them. All their history is our history, their inheritance is our inheritance and we share the same era; God's long era of salvation.

So the challenge for us is, as the Spirit of the Lord comes upon us, will we allow our lives, our era, to be absorbed into God's big era?

I love the words of this poem, attributed to Sir Francis Drake, which I think summaries the challenge before us.

Disturb us, Lord, when
We are too well pleased with ourselves,
When our dreams have come true
Because we have dreamed too little,
When we arrived safely
Because we sailed too close to the shore.
Disturb us, Lord, when
With the abundance of things we possess
We have lost our thirst
For the waters of life;
Having fallen in love with life,
We have ceased to dream of eternity

And in our efforts to build a new earth,
We have allowed our vision
Of the new heaven to dim.
Disturb us, Lord, to dare more boldly,
To venture on wider seas
Where storms will show your mastery;
Where losing sight of land, We shall find the stars.
We ask you to push back
The horizons of our hopes;
And to push into the future
In strength, courage, hope, and love

Image

We live in a world in which words summon up images in our minds. We mention 'apple' and perhaps in some cultures we sadly no longer think of a fruit but a computer or even a way of life. (I say this having just converted from a PC to a Mac!)

I'm aware that in mentioning the person and work of the Holy Spirit I conjure up a diversity of images in some people's minds. Some are good and some are wholesome, while others cause us to recoil due to past experiences. Some expressions of Christianity speak volumes about the Holy Spirit but seem very unattractive to us for many different reasons.

The true image of the Holy Spirit is Jesus Christ and the work of the Holy Spirit is the message of Jesus, so that should be enough to stop you backing off!

Jesus, the Son, came as the voice of the Father and the Spirit. So what we are really expecting when we submit to the work of the Holy Spirit is more of the person and presence of Jesus

Christ in our lives, relationships, boardrooms, on the streets, within legislation, and indeed anywhere that we are prepared to boldly go.

In a sense, this era of salvation that we have observed, from a human perspective, seems incredibly long. It runs from the birth and ministry of Jesus to an unspecified time in the future when he returns (Matthew 24:36).

It makes no difference to us whether Jesus returns sooner or later. Either way in this, our era, we have a part to play in his purposes.

Scripture causes me to believe that God's plan is for every generation of this era to say:

"The Spirit of the Lord is upon us. We have come to fulfil God's kingdom purposes in our lives and we will give everything to do it."

That's the declaration. I believe that's the challenge which, if embraced, will give us the heart from which we can really engage with all that's to come in the rest of this passage.

Yes, Jesus is the fulfilment – but not of concepts, ideologies, theologies or impersonal values. We can have a type of justice that is like an empty shell, but if we don't have the presence of Jesus at the heart we have missed the priceless pearl. Ultimately, this manifesto talks about a justice of both a temporal and eternal nature, and not just one or the other.

When we think 'Holy Spirit' we need to start thinking 'Jesus', when we think 'justice and liberation' we need to start thinking 'God's justice and liberation'.

How does the Holy Spirit work through Christ? I think at this stage it would help to look back into Isaiah 42:1-4, where we read about the Holy Spirit coming upon the Messiah. This is wonderful:

> *"Here is my servant whom I uphold,*
> *my chosen one in whom I delight;*
> *I will put my Spirit on him*
> *and he will bring justice to the nations.*
> *He will not shout or cry out,*
> *or raise his voice in the streets.*
> *A bruised reed he will not break,*
> *and a smouldering wick he will not snuff out.*
> *In faithfulness he will bring forth justice;*
> *he will not falter or be discouraged till he establishes justice on earth.*
> *In his law the islands will put their hope."*

The way of the Spirit is the way of Jesus. It is the way of power – holy power – the way of passion, the way of the anointing of God. However, it's not the way of comic book superheroes or powerful dominant celebrities. It is the way of suffering, the way of humility, the way of service. There's something very beautiful about the way Jesus outworks all of this in his life and relationships.

This is the challenge for us. If we want to be anointed by the Holy Spirit, if we want to flow in the Holy Spirit, how far are we willing to go? Are we willing to take the suffering as well as the glory? This is the challenge that lays at the beginning of the manifesto of Jesus.

Exodus God

Isaiah 61:1 introduces the Holy Spirit as the "Spirit of the sovereign Lord". Sovereign Lord is a divine title.

In Isaiah 50:4-7 we see this title "the sovereign Lord" repeated three times.

My favourite commentary on Isaiah is by Alec Motyer and is called *The Prophecy of Isaiah: An Introduction & Commentary*. It is absolutely excellent, and in it he observes that the sovereign Lord is the exodus God, the Saviour, the judge. He explores the link in the Jewish mind between the sovereign action of God and the exodus.

What this title declares is that we have an exodus God. If we want to understand what we're called to do, and what Jesus came to do, we need to look at the exodus. This is because the exodus is all about release from bondage, the release of slaves and the setting free of captives.

The sovereign act of God in the exodus affects individual people, changes a whole nation and affects a range of nations. That's what the exodus is all about. How amazing is that?

Why don't you take some time out right now and read the story in Exodus 12?

The reality is that the Jewish nation was liberated from Egypt due to the intervention of God, and for no other reason. God intervened, parting the waters, holding back the forces of the enemy, and bringing them through.

If we want to see God's work in people's lives, whether it's breaking the power of addiction, bringing physical healing, bringing emotional healing, seeing justice brought into our communities, seeing people released from the bondage of debt or seeing nations move into a better economic order, we need to see that all of this requires the power of the exodus God to be at work.

As churches we have an exodus calling to lead people out of bondage and slavery and into their inheritance. That's what our faith is about.

We are called to break the power of darkness over marriages, young people and children. We are called to bring freedom right to the heart of our society, to get a hold of people and say: "Let us take you out of slavery, let us show you what slavery you're in, and let us open up God's promised land. Come with us, we will take you into his future."

Sovereign Lord

This is what the sovereignty of God is all about.

God's sovereignty is not a vague, invisible force of "que sera sera, whatever will be will be".

It's his desire and ability to deliver a people out of slavery, and to use us as his exodus instruments so that he can display his amazing love and exodus power through his people.

The sovereignty of God is all about him choosing you, getting a hold of you and, in effect, saying: "I choose to open the way to all. If you respond to me you become part of my chosen people. If you respond to me I will get a hold of you and you will become my instrument.

The choice to respond is ours. As individuals, as a community and as the Church, will we respond? Will we understand that ultimately we are designed to be this community of the exodus, through whom God's sovereignty strangely moves?

Even though we are lacking in so many areas and at times we don't do things very well, or appear to not quite know what we're doing, God is with us. At times we lack the funding and we're not clever enough, bright enough, slick enough; we're not enough of anything!

Despite this, if the Spirit of the Lord is truly upon us, people will sense that there's something real and authentic there. It's the presence of the exodus God working through us in our weakness.

We've seen this time and time again. People from the locality working in social services or education have made comments to us like:

"What's different about you guys?" (Answer: Jesus!)

"You are serving, you know how to work in team, you've got a passion for the community, you're not just in your job for the money. You're not just about promotion, you're not about doing other people down. Why is this?" (Answer: Jesus!)

Here lays a bigger picture; it's that the Spirit of the Lord is present. It's with the anointing of the Spirit that God's works are done. We need to understand that the kingdom of God is not a static kingdom. It remains active only as the Holy Spirit continues to breathe life into lives, thoughts, actions, communities and structures.

In one sense it's inappropriate to have a company called "Kingdom Car Mechanics".

But the whole idea that this constitutes *the* kingdom just because we're Christians and following God is false thinking, biblically speaking.

The kingdom of God can't be institutionalised or owned. The kingdom comes as the Holy Spirit advents in our lives and creates a fruitful 'God moment'.

Someone may have an experience of the kingdom (Spirit) that provokes them to create a business repairing cars, which is inspired by the ethics of Jesus. These ethics begin to be expressed in working practices, which are clearly defined.

These working practices are a fruit of the kingdom and will only stay alive for the shelf life of the fruit. When the fruit begins to perish there needs to be a fresh crop, and this can only be supplied by the ongoing work of the Spirit. This will involve change and ongoing movement to keep in step with God's movements and not just our own agendas.

That's why, as churches, organisations and non-governmental organisations (NGOs), we need to watch out.

The further we get away from an encounter of the Spirit's refreshing, energising and renewing – both personally and corporately – the further we're getting away from the kingdom.

We can carry on, sometimes for years, on the basis of the fruit from the past, and historically most movements do. However, when this fruit finally perishes and we have no ongoing humble submission to the person and work of the Holy Spirit, we can end up left with a dying or dead mess! Even worse, experience and history show that this mess tends to get in the way of the next work that God initiates in the same sphere.

This is when churches and organisations begin to decline, and only a radical intervention from the Spirit at every level over a consistent period will be able to reverse this. Renewal is not only something that needs to happen to movements when they are in decline, however. Even the most vibrant organisations must recognise the need for continued renewal, even when it appears they are at the height of their powers. If they want to avoid an untimely demise, that is.

Sometimes the last thing we feel we need to do is respond to the Spirit of the Lord. It's challenging, disruptive, costly and so inconvenient. He is beyond our control.

When the Holy Spirit comes, often the first thing we experience is disruption. It's a challenge. Jesus' interjection of "I am the fulfilment" at the end of the passage was ultimately incredibly disruptive to the whole fabric of Jewish religious life and culture. But it was God breaking in.

We don't want our lives, organisations, trusts, budgets, businesses, church meetings or our church councils derailed. It's clear many of these have been carefully constructed in a way that ensures the Holy Spirit can't interrupt them!

If we back off at this stage we become prime candidates for decline, either on a personal or institutional level, or both. We begin to work in our own power and there is no doubt some great things can be done for God this way, for a season at least.

However, if we go with change, what happens then? Most likely we will get a big dose of disorder and a portion of chaos.

That's what happens when the Holy Spirit comes; many times things don't come together but begin to fall apart! The ministry of Jesus caused a massive interruption to the life of the 'believers' of the day. This caused tension and things had to change.

New wine requires new skins (Mark 2:21-22). The arrival of the Spirit in Jesus required a new skin to contain his people, both Jews and Gentiles, in the future. What he was doing at this time couldn't be contained within Judaism. This 'skin' was to be the new people of God, the Church.

This principle continues throughout every age and in many situations when the Spirit comes. Our lives start to change because suddenly we realise, "I'm no longer in control here. I need to hand over to the Lord, this seems chaotic!"

In reality, it only seems chaotic because new energy and new life is coming. My friend Jim McNeish observes that, "Our chaos is often God's order."

When you are in the middle of a traffic jam it seems chaotic, but when the same event is observed by helicopter from overhead you can see the wave patterns of traffic movements. This reveals a symmetry that cannot be identified in the heat of the jam.

Most dynamic churches and organisations learn to embrace the new and hold through the chaos. If you hold onto it securely a new order generally emerges out of chaos. The pattern God is working becomes more obvious, but this takes time to perceive.

Once we allow the Holy Spirit to come this new order arrives and is characterised by fresh life and not the old stale fruit.

At the beginning we can be afraid of what we might lose. When the Holy Spirit comes to you or your organisation what might you lose?

Why are we afraid of really letting God move? Are we concerned about losing control by allowing the Holy Spirit free reign? Are we worried about our credibility or concerned about what God may ask of us?

If we focus on God we come to realise that all we have to lose is what's past and all we have to gain is Christ and his future. In any case, none of us is really in control - although we live under the constant pressure of trying to control everything!

There was something within me that really loved the Icelandic volcanic ash cloud that grounded air travel across the world. Once my focus moved away from friends trapped in far-flung corners of the earth, I began to see that there's much to be learned from this phenomenon.

One main lesson is that, with all our technology and knowhow, we were powerless to resolve this. With a few 'puffs' the culture and technology of the world grinds to a halt. We just had to wait and hope that the eruption would cease and that the wind would change direction.

I was reminded of Psalm 19:1-4:

> *The heavens declare the glory of God;*
> *the skies proclaim the work of his hands.*
> *Day after day they pour forth speech;*
> *night after night they display knowledge.*
> *There is no speech or language where their voice is not heard.*
> *Their voice goes out into all the earth,*
> *their words to the end of the world.*

Creation reflects God's awesome power and glory and it 'speaks' to us! The problem is, not many appear to be listening!

Creation's volcanic nature is part of what keeps the earth alive and, as humans, we have to work around that and should respect it. We are part of creation and therefore our prosperity is bound up with its abundance. We are called to 'care' for creation; we are both part of creation and made in God's image. At the same time we are dwarfed by the power of creation and should be humbled by the intricate beauty and loveliness of nature, which speaks to us very clearly and says: *"You are not in control!"*

Sociologists have estimated that we have no way of controlling around 85% of life's circumstances and events. It's this 85% that many of us get so stressed about. We must recognise we are at the mercy of the 'elements'. That's where faith comes in.

Those with faith are not necessarily those that are able to give the appearance of a 'God-like' control over their lives and circumstances. Faith gives us confidence, flexibility and access to the presence and activity of God, which enables us to successfully navigate the 'volcanic unpredictabilities' of life. Faith loosens us up and empowers us to focus on what we can determine rather than stressing about the 85% we cannot.

This remaining 15% of our lives requires our urgent attention. We can strongly influence it through our choices, actions and responses to events around us. On top of this, even though we are unable to prevent some things happening or change past events, we can choose how we frame them in our minds and how we choose to respond to them. This will dramatically affect how we feel in the present and who we become in the future.

The challenge to us as we stand before God and respond to Jesus is to allow him to be Lord, to welcome the uncertainty and risk of being filled with God's Spirit and then embark on the wonderful, scary journey of following in the footsteps of Jesus Christ. We don't have the power to 'make it happen', we cannot predict what will come our way, but we can ensure that we are focused and anchored in obedience to the core essential message of Jesus, that we are 'centred' in the right place.

Presence now!

In Matthew 12:22-37 Jesus talks about the coming of the Holy Spirit.

Jesus is demonstrating the power of the Holy Spirit and the arrival of God's kingdom in him by performing miracles, signs and wonders. As usual, the religious people (Pharisees) don't get on very well with it; they hated it.

They accuse him of casting out demons by demonic means, but Jesus puts them straight. He basically says: "Look, it can't be the devil because what kingdom can survive if it's divided? If I drive out demons by the Spirit of God then the kingdom of God has come to you."

Some translations talk about the finger of God – meaning the touch of God, the presence of God. I believe this is what we should be looking for if we want to be able to respond effectively to the manifesto of Jesus.

God's imminent intervention in our lives comes at the school gate, in the business meeting, in the city and in our universities. The question is, where is the Spirit of God moving?

Allowing the Holy Spirit to continually move in our lives, our budgets, our trusts, our relationships, our marriages, our friends and our communities opens the door for his work of bringing liberation, reign and rule, deliverance, healing and good news to every sphere of society and culture.

So I hope we start this book by coming to a place where we can say, "The Spirit of the sovereign Lord is upon me". Not because we're as good as Jesus, nor because we are stupidly arrogant, but because Jesus has been there before us, and he's done it; he's paved the way. He's been to the cross, he's risen from the dead, he's ascended to be at the right hand of the Father, and he's sent the Holy Spirit so we can say, "The Spirit of the sovereign Lord is upon me".

As the Church we can say, "The Spirit of the sovereign Lord is upon us. Look out community, here we come!" God is looking for an anointed people and an anointed community. He's not looking for superstars, he's looking for a body, a family and a community that he can fill.

Jesus Christ is our model:

"Who being in very nature God did not consider equality with God something to be grasped, but made himself nothing, taking the very nature of a servant" (Philippians 2:6-7).

Jesus totally submitted to the will of the Father and to the impulse of the Spirit as he led him into the business of God's manifesto. It was his core and his passion, so it should also be ours.

POSTCARDS FROM MY FRIENDS — LUKE SMITH

Luke is a great guy who works for Fusion, a brilliant work among students that I was involved in setting up, although it is now led by my friend Rich Wilson. Luke is a fantastic example of a young leader who 'keeps it real' but will step out in faith with God. This story is about listening to God, seeing his presence at work in our lives and not being afraid to live outside the box. Over to Luke:

The thing that excites me most about Jesus is that he is real! This gospel that millions of people simply pay homage to around the globe really is a world-changing truth with the power to save and transform lives. It's not all hype, its real – and this is worth giving everything up for.

Everything needs interpreting, right? Nothing is literal, surely. That is what I thought when God gave me a vision of myself in a cage, with a mate, outside York Minster. What was the deep significance and symbolism behind this strange image? After a couple of months I realised that God was not being cryptic. He actually wanted me to get in a cage, with a mate, outside York Minster. So I did.

We called it the Cage of Freedom. For a whole week, my friend Gavin Loftus and I spent every hour of the day in there. We spent 168 hours in a cage right outside our church (St Michael le Belfrey) next to York Minster. We stood there, sat there, went to the toilet there and slept there – for a week. It was just eight feet long and four feet wide.

The aim of this prophetic stunt was to speak to as many people as possible about Jesus and the freedom he gives. We also offered to pray for people. Taking inspiration from St Paul who said, "Though I am free and belong to no-one, I have made myself a slave to everyone, to win as many as possible" (1 Corinthians 9: 19), we set out to imprison ourselves for a week. We put ourselves in the hands of the city of York and the living God.

Against the advice of others, we decided to live by faith for food while in the cage. We brought only a bottle of water into the cage with us, trusting that God would meet our needs during our visit. We were also trusting God to keep us safe in what was the most vulnerable situation either of us have ever faced.

When the key clicked the lock shut, a surge of blood coursed through my veins and made me shudder. This was it. I was terrified and invigorated at the same time. I had no idea whether this would work. We might get attacked. I thought God had told me to do it, but there is always an element of risk in obeying God. What if I had just made it up? We prayed this prayer: "God, if we are just being idiots and are doing something stupid, then take these idiots and their stupid gift and use it for your glory." A peace rushed into us.

Our concerns that the cage might be ignored were not founded in reality. We were very quickly surrounded by about 20 lads on a stag night, a scene that we would get used to. One guy hurled abuse, another laughed and another spat. But one engaged in a really good discussion with us for about twenty minutes while four of his friends listened. Then they all moved on. In that short time, I had probably talked about Jesus to someone who didn't know him for longer than in whole of the previous year put together, and this was only the start.

As the week went on we personally spoke to more than two thousand people about Jesus, his love for them and the freedom he offers us when we feel trapped. Thousands more spoke to our friends on the outside of the cage and even more read our signs on the cage that talked about the same freedom. Three people gave their lives to Jesus while talking to us through the bars of the cage.

Somewhere in the region of fifty people came and asked for prayer. I prayed with a man who had lost the respect of his family. Gav prayed for a teenage mum who had just lost custody of her kids. A family of five asked me to pray for them as the dad had just come out of prison and off drugs and they all wanted help. God just kept bringing people who needed to experience his peace and freedom.

One evening a large gentleman of about sixty came to the cage. He said: "Look lads, I don't believe in God and I have never said a prayer. But my best friend died today and I don't know what to do and it says on your sign that you will pray. So will you pray?" He then bowed his head. Taken aback, we prayed a simple prayer that God would give the man his peace and thanked God for his friend's life. He looked up and he was shining. He burst into tears and couldn't stop thanking us saying, "I've never felt like this. I feel so light and free."

I explained to him that he had received the peace of God's Spirit and assured him that he would sleep really well. I suggested that he go home, rest and come back the next day if he wanted to talk about it more. He did come back the next day, and every day after that. He has now joined our cell group and comes to church with us.

It never failed to amuse and astound us how irritated and angry atheists became when they saw the cage. One morning, as I washed my feet in a small bowl, a well-dressed man in his fifties came up to the cage. Without a greeting he said: "I am so irritated that you are here." Struggling to hold back the laughter, I asked him why he thought that was. He was sure that it was because of my attempt to "shove God down his throat". He could not be tranquilised by my observation that I was washing my feet and he was shouting at me, so how could I be shoving God anywhere? God is real and he is often more present to those who deny him than to those who ignore him.

I can recommend living by faith for food as well. My word, how God provided! He kept providing throughout the week. In fact, he provided in such abundance that we had to give away 90% of all that we were given. The vast majority was given by complete strangers who came over and chatted to us. Some people loved what we were doing and others hated it, but they still brought food back for us. We ended up just asking people to leave it on the outside of the cage in a pile, which we shared with anyone who came to chat to us. This is how God's economy works. We went into the cage with nothing to give and gave more that week than ever before. You don't need stuff to be able to give; you just need a heart to give.

Among many others, we shared our food with a homeless guy called Jacko. He was our neighbour for the week as he lived in a bush about twenty yards from our cage. It was a pleasure to get to know him throughout the week and his jokes made us chuckle on many occasions. He noticed that we prayed a lot and that we were given a lot of food. On agreeing with his observations, I asked him what his favourite food in the whole world was. He scratched his dirty beard, then said in a raspy voice: "Mr Kipling's almond slices".

So we prayed with him: "God, please provide some Mr Kipling's almond slices because our friend Jacko really loves them, you love him and we want him to know it." Half an hour later, a portly man cycled up to the cage and out of the basket on his bike he removed some Mr Kipling's almond slices. When we asked him about them, he said that he wasn't a Christian but had seen what we were doing through Facebook and had decided to visit us. Half an hour before he was in a supermarket and thought he would buy us some food, and that is what he settled on! Jacko thought it was a set-up, but when he realised it was genuine he was moved.

I am still friends with Jacko. It was a privilege to have him for dinner at our house after I got out of the cage. He had his first bath for four months, after which I shaved his face and gave him new clothes. This is the closest I have come to understanding what Jesus meant when he said: "For I was hungry and you gave me something to eat, I was thirsty and you gave me something to drink, I was a stranger and you invited me in, I needed clothes and you clothed me, I was sick and you looked after me, I was in prison and you came to visit me." (Matthew 25:35-36). Again, I learned not to look for the deep symbolism in what Jesus said and dared to take it as truth.

One of the most bizarre incidents in the cage happened at eleven pm on the Friday evening. An angry man came up to the cage shouting in a strong Yorkshire accent, "Where's my bike?" We told him we didn't know and when he asked us what we were doing we told him we were telling people about Jesus. This really wound He yelled, "What good is that to me? I've had my bike stolen from next to your cage!"

Just then, a friend of ours from church arrived and on hearing this he said, "I think I know where your bike is". He took him over to a wall about thirty yards from the cage and, to the irate man's surprise, pointed at the bike in question. It was unharmed and its broken lock was propped on top of it. This totally baffled everyone. The man came back to the cage and kept asking us: "What's happened here? What are you doing here?"

With a lot of laughter, we repeatedly assured him that we had no idea what had happened to his bike, but that we had been telling people about Jesus all evening and seemingly someone had tried to steal his bike and failed to do so. He stayed and chatted for a long time. Then he cycled home, got into bed, got out of bed, cycled back to the cage and asked us again, "What happened again?" When God breaks into someone's life, it is such an irritant it can't be ignored.

Before getting into the cage, I had promised my amazing wife Hannah that if I felt I was going to break psychologically, I would get out of the cage. I almost reached that stage a few times. After twenty-four hours I was claustrophobic, we had received a lot of abuse and it was very hot. My stomach felt like it was tied in knots. I gave God five minutes to do something or I was getting out of the cage.

Literally thirty seconds later some people I had never set eyes on before came up and asked who Luke was. Disbelievingly, I put my hand up and they said they had been sent with some flapjack and love from someone who was praying for me. It turned out to be my aunty in St Albans. I burst into tears at the direct answer to prayer and the feeling of being so close to God's will.

There were some harrowing times involving drunks, aggressive blokes and some demonic people. But Jesus had authority over all of these people. Our faith in this grew drastically over the week. In front of a group of people, I pointed at a man who was shouting obscenities about the Church and God and instructed him to be silent in the name of Jesus. He was struck mute. I have never seen anything like it.

Another night, we lay in the cage as a group of revellers shouted, kicked and shook the cage. We both fell asleep through this, dwelling on the story of Jesus calming the storm when the disciples panicked. Jesus was in our boat that night, so we slept. God also provided us with a guardian angel called Andy. He was a night porter who finished work at midnight and sat on a bench near the cage from midnight to six am every night. What a hero and man of God.

I hope that this story of my week in the Cage of Freedom encourages people who know Jesus well enough to believe in him fully and dare to believe that his words are true. The gospel is just as attractive and repellent as it has ever been. It still transforms lives. It still offends. If we are seeing fewer people come to faith in Jesus, it is not the fault of the gospel. We have probably just lost our bottle.

A final reflection is that I believe the cage worked because we made ourselves vulnerable and put the power in the hands of those on the outside. This made people feel safe, so they felt that they could come and ask us what we were doing. We could answer, but they could walk away when they chose and we were trapped. I believe we can learn from this is our daily lives. God works out of our weakness not our strength.

CHAPTER 2:

GOOD NEWS

As we look again at this passage we will see the common thread of 'good news' that runs through it. To my mind it's good news to those who need it most.

Luke 4:17-21

> *The scroll of the prophet Isaiah was handed to him. Unrolling it, he found the place where it is written:*
>
> *"The Spirit of the sovereign Lord is on me, because he has anointed me to preach good news to the poor.*
> *He has sent me to proclaim freedom for the prisoners*
> *and recovery of sight for the blind,*
> *to release the oppressed, to proclaim the year of the Lord's favour."*
>
> *Then he rolled up the scroll, gave it back to the attendant and sat down. The eyes of everyone in the synagogue were fastened on him, and he began by saying to them, "Today, this Scripture is fulfilled in your hearing."*

This passage is the essence of what being a follower of Jesus Christ is all about. He is the fulfilment of the Old Testament prophetic hope for a Messiah. The Spirit of the Lord is upon Jesus and this Holy Spirit is the key and exclusive agent for God's work in our lives and upon the earth.

As a result, it's impossible to receive the kingdom of God other than through the Holy Spirit, so perhaps it's wise to think about how we can connect more with the Spirit's work. The great news is that the Spirit of God is active everywhere, and is not confined to the Church, just as the kingdom, reign and rule of God is far more expansive than the people of God.

God's Spirit tends to hang out with people and pop up in situations that are far outside our religious boxes. God's kingdom, is 'out there' as well as 'in here'. So if there is goodness, love, forgiveness and justice occurring anywhere, you can be certain that the Holy Spirit is not too far away.

There's something organic, Holy Spirit-catalysed and powerful about the kingdom of God. Therefore, when we get to talking about transformation, justice and the working lives of our communities and organisations, we need to be anchored in the real life of God. Because it's the life of God that will bring about the transformation, keeping things fresh and real.

Where next?

So, what is our message? Well, the essence of the message is that there is good news for the poor. It's good news for those who need it most. It's good news about the cross, the resurrection of Jesus, salvation and the reign and rule of God. It can be touched and tasted now. It's heaven coming to earth now. It's a foretaste of glory. But what is this like? The rest of this book will put some flesh on the bones.

This kingdom comes in many different ways including healing, justice and care for the poor. It arrives in education, in the arts or just within legislation. It advents in the life of an individual as they find Jesus as Lord and Saviour and begin to live his way, tasting the life of the age to come. It touches earth in the relief of poverty through the provision of resources, employment or the means of breaking people free from the chains of the poverty trap. Every experience of God now is a foretaste of when heaven comes to earth in fullness.

The good news of Jesus is that we're not going to heaven, heaven is coming to us. (If you would like to explore this train of thought more fully I would recommend a book called *Surprised by Hope* by NT Wright).

This passage causes us to pose the question, who are the poor? On one level, we should realise that no-one could stand before the creator of the universe who is all holiness, all goodness, totally resplendent, full of light, full of glory, all-powerful and all-knowing and say, "Hey, I'm not poor!"

As human beings we stand before this glorious God and we have to admit that we are all poor by comparison. Therefore, this message of good news is for every human being.

The religious people of the day were scandalised by the company that Jesus kept and were indignant at his association with people they viewed as the unholy and unclean. These were people they were unwilling to engage with as they wanted to hang on to their outward, ritual cleanness. Eat with the wrong types and your worship at the temple could be impeded according to their interpretation of the holy life. The Messiah,

God among them, had something else in mind!

Matthew 9:9-13 says:

> *As Jesus went on from there, he saw a man named Matthew sitting at the tax collector's booth. "Follow me," he told him, and Matthew got up and followed him.*
>
> *While Jesus was having dinner at Matthew's house, many tax collectors and 'sinners' came and ate with him and his disciples. When the Pharisees saw this, they asked his disciples, "Why does your teacher eat with tax collectors and 'sinners'?"*
>
> *On hearing this, Jesus said, "It is not the healthy who need a doctor, but the sick. But go and learn what this means: 'I desire mercy, not sacrifice.' For I have not come to call the righteous, but sinners."*

As Jesus spoke he exposed the pride, arrogance and stupidity of the religious. He expressed God's intolerance of empty religion and at the same time the openness and love of God to all who are open and humble before him. Jesus came for those who understand their human sinfulness and have a sober assessment of the human condition, not for those who think they already have it all together and believe they can make it by their own means.

However, we now begin to see that the understanding that every human being is poor without God simply provides context. As we engage more deeply we see that Jesus is talking about the literal poor, as well as those of us, like me, who are not in physical poverty, but are bankrupt anyway without God's ongoing grace and generosity.

This is a holistic passage that has an ongoing interplay between both the literal and metaphorical, and we will see this rhythm at work through every line.

Here we are confronted by the heart of God for the poor, which is revealed throughout the Bible. We are challenged by the big picture, but as we look at Jesus we see that he lived his message every day alongside those who were closest to him.

We might ask, "Who are our poor?" If God has given us good news and a message, who do we take it to? Who are the poor that we can touch, that are within our reach, in our locale?

Whose names are we carrying in our hearts and minds – who are the people around about us that we are praying for? What communities do our churches, businesses and families carry in terms of prayer, serving and giving?

Who are our poor?

Several years ago Maggie was in church leadership, leading the central congregation of our church, yet as she had prayed and focused on Scripture she felt the impulse of God pulling her toward the poor. This was the context that our American friend spoke into prophetically without prior knowledge.

As we talked together she just said: "Look, I feel God is calling me. I'm asking the question, I'm praying 'who are the poor for me?'"

At that stage we'd had a number of people in our church who had encountered sexual abuse and one of our young leaders, a seventeen-year-old girl, had been raped on her way back from a meeting.

She was absolutely devastated. Maggie sat with her, talked to her, and realised she just didn't have the expertise to help. This girl went to the doctor. The doctor gave her a phone number for a crisis centre thirty miles away that wouldn't take her because she was outside their area. The only alternative was a psychiatric hospital. Maggie was appalled by this situation and felt we were witnessing a human rights atrocity right under our noses.

Those who had been victims of sexual violence became her 'poor' and a long journey began towards the outworking of this new-found passion.

I believe that these words of Jesus call us all to a similar journey, a journey that all of us as communities and individuals need to travel. We need to ask that question, who are our poor?

In the words of Christian activist and communicator Shane Claiborne, "the poor will always have a name". They're not just an anonymous group of people out there.

The next chapter explores the intimate and personal nature of this passage. It's about individuals – people with names. People who are our friends, people we journey with, people we love. This manifesto is full of love for humanity.

This is wonderful because it describes a spirituality that is both internal and outward-facing. It's a spirituality that's completely holistic. It's not dualistic. There's no dichotomy between bodily behaviour (earthly), and spiritual activity (heavenly), between the sacred and the secular, between prayer and action. We see that in the life of Jesus the only truly secular thing is sin. Everything else comes under the influence of his manifesto and is the domain of the Holy Spirit, who wants to bring 'new creation' by way of restoration and freedom.

Suddenly we realise there's no such thing as a secular job and that we need be no less spiritual when working than when praying. The whole of our lives are called to be worship, orientated towards serving and obeying God.

However, the worship we express as we gather as Christians to pray and celebrate together is vitally important. It has a unique and crucial role. It's intended to connect us to God, instruct and equip us, giving impetus and resources towards outworking the manifesto, both individually and together.

Internal and external

The very nature of this manifesto is 'good news'. The words "good news" or "gospel" mean "a message of victory which is in essence liberating to all".

Within our culture we are naturally cynical and suspicious of good news. The most successful newspapers and magazines are those that peddle bad news about people, and every new exposé guarantees a surge in sales. However, I believe that deep down inside we long for hope, for a future and for a power that brings with it something other than the endless drudgery and hopelessness of life without purpose. Well this is it; the message of the Saviour, the saviour of the whole of humanity who can become our saviour if we make room for him in our lives.

The good news Jesus talks about is freedom for prisoners, recovery of sight for the blind and release for the oppressed. These are both internal and external. Within the Church we have those who focus on 'signs and wonders' and feel that others who are concerned with justice are unspiritual and perhaps 'fleshly' - working in their own strength.

At the same time, you have those focused on justice who see the others as irrelevant, immersed in the Christian ghetto and separated from both the real world and the real concerns of God. As we look at the words and life of Jesus, however, we do not see this dichotomy. We see one message, one kingdom, one gospel and one lifestyle. These two sides of the same coin are intended to ride in tandem together rather than travelling on separate journeys.

I believe those that are involved in justice and social transformation can give people who are passionate about the miraculous something relevant to pray for, prophesy over and seek the miraculous in. This is a possible alternative to being preoccupied with personal experiences and religious irrelevancies that have little or no impact on the world Jesus came to redeem.

Similarly, those that are passionate about intercession and prayer can work with others who are involved in issues of justice who sometimes feel overwhelmed and powerless, as if they are carrying the burdens of the world. Prayer and the prophetic can take situations into the presence of God, unlock God's life and bring growth in unique ways; ways that no board, strategic plan, financial clout or pure hard work are able to achieve.

Here a potentially world-changing synergy emerges and many times over the last twenty years, in my experience, the progress of NGOs and major campaigns against injustice have mysteriously shifted up a gear as the energy and action of the activists was soaked in the prayers and intercession of the mystics. By mystics I mean those whose Christian faith is more rooted in prayer, reflection, the prophetic and a supernatural lens than it is in activism. The message of Jesus blurs the boundaries and draws the activist towards the invisible realms of prayer, while at the same time empowering the mystically inclined to have a go at becoming the answer and fulfilment of their prayers and visions.

Furthermore, being directed by Jesus and his message can keep both mystics and activists rooted. Mystics are harnessed and prevented from falling off the edge of reality, and activists are protected, being kept centred in a relational encounter with the living God, who is their true source.

As we journey this way we realise that the prophetic ministry post-Jesus is intended to be yoked to his message and purposes, and the whole emphasis of prayer is intended to be aligned to the kingdom of God as we pray, "Your kingdom come, your will be done on earth as it is in heaven" (Matthew 6: 9-10).

The Christian life was never intended to be contained within a self-sustaining subculture but is designed to be lived out in the full glare of mainstream culture, shining like a light into the darkness.

Just reflect for a moment on the difference between a wild lion and a lion in a zoo. You visit the zoo and you look at the lion lying there in the cage. It's almost like he's saying: "I've not killed for some while, I'm a little fat, I'll just lay here as the next meal will soon come to me, then I'll die."

I always feel so sad for these creatures that have become such a poor reflection of their majestic potential. They are *wild*life, made for the wild.

On the other hand, should you visit a game reserve, wind down your window and look into the eyes of a passing lion you realise there's only one thing that's going through his mind: "Dinner! Give me a chance and I'm going to eat you!"

This wild creature is in his element, a king, the top of the food chain and a force to be reckoned with.

This kingdom message is designed for the wild, for the great outdoors and not for the inside. That's where it comes alive and that's where we are destined to follow in the footsteps of Jesus.

For example, this good news brings freedom from debt: monetary, relational and even spiritual debt. Jesus is bringing in a new economy where at last we realise that real healing and wholeness involve liberation from both the chains of our sin and also our physical debts. The slate is wiped clean.

Christian discipleship is the process by which the freedom we receive in the Holy Spirit is earthed into the reality of our lives through obedience, discipline and the support of those around us. We also begin to pass on this good news to others and help them follow in our footsteps as we follow Jesus.

This good news is freedom from our emptiness as human beings. It's freedom and forgiveness of sin so that the decks can be cleared for relationship with God. It's release from fear.

But what happens next? Now what? Without fear, those whose fear has stopped them from working are now bold enough to go and get a job. They are no longer bound by the oppression of the past but can now be the people they were created to be. They can pay off debts, even pay off someone else's debts, because sin has been forgiven by God, and fear has been taken from their hearts.

Salvation is simultaneously an internal event, an economic event and an event with relational, social and environmental consequences. The new relationship with God transforms all relationships. It's reconciliation between God and humanity, in human relationships and between humanity and creation. This is the practice of 'spirituality', Jesus style.

This process works the other way round, as reflected by organisations such as Christians against Poverty (CAP), which works to support and advise people as to how they can navigate their way out of financial debt. Their story would be that many people, as they experience the good news of freedom from financial debt, have asked the 'why' question of CAP and have found faith in Jesus Christ during the process. It starts with a taste of the good news and suddenly the door is open to the whole feast.

As churches we must realise how powerful our gifts are. This includes gifts to local agencies, food parcels, money put through letterboxes and time attending to the practical needs of our communities. When the anonymous and quiet cries of the lonely, which are often only heard by God, are heard by God's people and met by material gifts given via God's network – his Church – then the message rings out loud and clear: "Freedom comes via the good news of Jesus".

Biblical spirituality and holiness cover both the visible and invisible realms, both the external and the internal, both the intents of the heart and the actions of the body.

Why not pause for a moment and read Matthew 5; you will see Jesus clearly explaining this. How radical, beautiful and inspiring are his words?

The spiritual realm is not merely an invisible realm. It's not about a realm divorced from the physical. When the Holy Spirit comes he becomes intertwined with the human, the emotional and the physical. Yes, he operates beyond our physical perception at times, but the spiritual realm encompasses the physical. In this life there is no separation between the two.

This is why the apostle warns that a prophet's words are subject to human limitations and weaknesses so are never pure revelation (1 Corinthians 13:9). He also points out that, despite the fact that at times our experience of God might be ecstatic and involve an altered state, it's still subject to the will and control of the prophet. So no-one can say "God made me do it!" (Acts 10:10). Although Peter falls into a "trance" which is ecstatic in nature according to Paul in 1 Corinthians 14:32, this is not an experience that overrides his self-control.

Holistic

Jesus talks about sight for the blind and in his ministry opened the eyes of the blind.

Matthew 11:2-6:

> *When John heard in prison what Christ was doing, he sent his disciples to ask him, "Are you the one who was to come, or should we expect someone else?"*
>
> *Jesus replied, "Go back and report to John what you hear and see: the blind receive sight, the lame walk, those who have leprosy*

are cured, the deaf hear, the dead are raised, and the good news is preached to the poor. Blessed is the man who does not fall away on account of me."

Jesus had demonstrated his messianic credentials and at the same time was modelling the miraculous nature of the kingdom of God.

Blind to spiritual reality

He is clearly declaring that those who are spiritually blinded will have their eyes opened to God.

The testimony of human history is that we are unable to see and know God through our own efforts. Even in our most enlightened state, with all the testimony of nature and the intelligence of the species, we are trapped in the dark. We are blind and unable to save ourselves.

But Jesus comes to bring sight to the blind, addressing an immediate spiritual need for every human being.

John 3:1-9:

> *Now there was a man of the Pharisees named Nicodemus, a member of the Jewish ruling council. He came to Jesus at night and said, "Rabbi, we know you are a teacher who has come from God. For no-one could perform the miraculous signs you are doing if God were not with him."*
>
> *In reply, Jesus declared, "I tell you the truth, no one can see the kingdom of God unless he is born again."*
>
> *"How can a man be born when he is old?" Nicodemus asked. "Surely he cannot enter a second time into his mother's womb to be born!"*

Jesus answered, "I tell you the truth, no one can enter the kingdom of God unless he is born of water and the Spirit. Flesh gives birth to flesh, but the Spirit gives birth to spirit. You should not be surprised at my saying, 'You must be born again.' The wind blows wherever it pleases. You hear its sound, but you cannot tell where it comes from or where it is going. So it is with everyone born of the Spirit."

My wife's grandfather was a missionary in China before the Communist regime came to power and he was a medical doctor. He would go with a small team into a village, find a community building and set up a hospital centre.

Here they would invite all the people with cataracts to come and he would prepare to operate on them. Before the surgery he would read this passage, particularly the verses about the good news of Jesus being sight to the blind.

He performed operations on all the cataracts, give people back their sight, and then tell them about how Jesus could deal with the greater problem of all humanity - the need for spiritual sight. How good is that?!

These missionaries knew how to suffer and follow in the footsteps of Jesus. They were separated from their children, who were in a missionary school which became a concentration camp as the Communists began to gain ground. My wife's mother Elizabeth, the daughter of this surgeon, was in this camp with her brothers and sisters. They ended up marooned in appalling conditions for more than six years (her account can be found in *God Can Be Trusted* by Elizabeth Goldsmith). Meanwhile, their parents were on the other side of China. Their mother contracted typhoid and all her husband could do, without the necessary drugs, was nurse her as she died. Elizabeth and her brothers and sisters never saw their mother again.

In the 1990s, Elizabeth went back to China and visited the village where her parents had been based. There she met a woman who is now leading a church of over a thousand people, and this woman gave a testimony along these lines:

> *I used to baby-sit for you when you were a child. Do you know that your parents didn't see many convert to Christ when they were here, just a handful of us, but they taught us how to suffer? We watched them weep, we watched them die, we watched them bury their loved ones and we watched them mourn. When Communism came, we knew how to survive because we had learned to suffer from them and those of us that stayed faithful through the Communist regime are now leaders in this new revival. Your parents laid the foundation for this move of God that is now in full swing."*

What a wonderful thing to hear. The things that we sometimes sow in tears will be reaped in joy by others. This kingdom message is a message that, in the fullness of time, will change nations.

Jesus proclaims freedom and release for prisoners and modelled this in many ways. Bringing release to the woman caught in adultery (John 8:1-11), to those held captive by demonic powers (Mark 5:1-20) and to those subject to the prison of racism or religious prejudice (the Good Samaritan - Luke 10:25-37).

It could be asserted that casting a Samaritan in the good role within this parable is both politically and socially subversive. It would perhaps be the equivalent of reinterpreting it as the parable of the 'Good Muslim' from the viewpoint of the church that planned ritual Koran burning in the US in 2010!

I have encountered many examples over the years of people who have come into the orbit of church life who have been clearly demonically oppressed. I remember one occasion when a mother from a family with no obvious Christian faith sought me out. Her daughter had been involved in the occult via a Ouija board and had since become paranoid, experienced all sorts of unpleasant physical manifestations and could not sleep. Her GP was unable to help. After one prayer the daughter was totally set free which resulted in her, the mother and eventually her brother becoming followers of Jesus. Good news certainly came to their whole family.

This gospel brings release from inner fears, the power of evil forces and evil which manifests itself in the unjust structures of our world. As the good news is proclaimed and received it will both transform individuals and change systems. It releases us so that we can accept ourselves and find personal peace and fulfilment. But it's also about release from physical prisons. It's about campaigning on behalf of those who are unjustly imprisoned.

I remember years ago, before the breakdown of the Iron Curtain, going to the then Soviet Union. We were undertaking an audit for a charity that was campaigning on behalf of those who were in prison. We met several families of Christians who were in prison for their faith. Our job was to help keep track of who was in prison so they would not be forgotten and to provide a basis for various campaigns.

We took a variety of items that could be sold on the black market for food, as many of the people were starving. I went through customs with a case full of women's underwear and computer equipment, among other things!

One of the most touching moments was sitting with a Jewish family. We had no shared language, just a dictionary. We sat together and connected through faltering communication, slowly gathering information. There was very limited scope for verbal communication and yet our shared humanity and human connection made room for the presence of God to enter the room. The connection of love and appreciation was tangible and the one word we shared together was "Halleluia".

God's kingdom is about release in every area.

The spiritual realm

The Bible is not dualistic. Both our inner lives and physical lives are intended to be filled with the freedom of this good news.

1 Corinthians 6:19 states:

"Do you not know that your body is a temple of the Holy Spirit, who is in you, whom you have received from God?"

Our immediate reaction to this is to think about the 'Holy Spirit' and the invisible. But how we behave physically cannot be separated from our spiritual lives. One will surely affect the other. This is a message to those who believe they can behave immorally sexually without affecting their spiritual state. This is not possible.

But let's look at this from another angle for a moment. What is the verse saying? Your body is a temple. The body is important.

We should look after our bodies because the physical realm is also spiritual. 'Spiritual' people are not those who flagellate and abuse their bodies, it's about looking after God's temple. This means self-control and at times restraint, because not everything that is permissible is beneficial to our wellbeing (1 Corinthians 6:12; 10:23). Being 'spiritual' biblically is not retreating into a subjective realm, which can only be enjoyed by those who have the 'revelation'. It's about being more like Jesus, who was the supreme example of a human being.

How should you behave in a sacred temple? You wouldn't go in with muddy boots, put dirty hands all over precious artefacts and throw rubbish everywhere, unless of course you wanted to be arrested or thrown out!

Generally, we would behave with respect, care and reverence. So we should treat our bodies and the bodies of others with respect. When we look at the physical world, we should look at it through the eyes of love, because God created it and the good news brings God's freedom and liberation to all of creation; both the physical and invisible realms.

I welcome the emphasis within the teaching of NT Wright. In *Surprised by Hope* he emphasises the physical nature of the resurrection, that the hope we anticipate is that of a physical new heaven and a new earth.

Likewise, this passage does not exclusively spiritualise the good news. It's an earthly, physical, tangible message. Because being 'in the Spirit' is not about being off somewhere, on some other planet, neither is being 'fleshly' about being practically aware or rooted in your humanity. Jesus demonstrated this in his incarnation, becoming fully human as well as being fully God.

The resurrection body of Jesus was still fully physical as he was touched by Thomas (John 20:27-8) and enjoyed a fish supper with Peter (John 21:11-15), even if it was more flexible than his body prior to the resurrection in some interesting ways (John 20:19-23)!

When some translations of the Bible contrast being 'in the flesh' and 'in the Spirit', what they are really referring to is not the visible versus the invisible. It's that which is animated by life outside of God versus that which is energised by the Spirit of God, be it visible or invisible.

It's that which is animated merely by human effort divorced from the grace of God and life of the Spirit versus human efforts energised by the grace of God and lived in the life of the Spirit. It's acting in independence and arrogance towards God rather than in partnership, humility and through faith in God.

Sometimes we are led and influenced by things that are outside of God's heart, such as greed, independence, self-interest and our own agendas. When our lives are animated by those things, we are 'in the flesh', as some would say. Our deeds may even be objectively good but are dead because the life and heart of God is not in them.

However, I dislike the term 'flesh' as it can lead to wrong assumptions. Some give the impression that rational thinking, righteous deeds, love in action, relationships, obedient acts and enjoying the physical gifts God gives is somehow less 'spiritual' than having some kind of 'secret and mystical experience' or living a life that withdraws from art, beauty, culture, academia and the physical realm.

This at times can border on Gnosticism, which is not just incredibly damaging to the gospel of Jesus, it's also damaging to humanity and the image of God seen in Jesus Christ, the second Adam who has a resurrection body (1Corinthians 15:45).

The hope for the future beyond death and when the kingdom of God comes in fullness is not of a disembodied and unreal future but a new kind of physicality where this current realm is swallowed up by God's glory and transformed (1 Corinthians 15:35-58).

Being 'in the Spirit' is a term that I like a lot more than 'in the flesh'. It's about our whole lives being energised by the values of the Holy Spirit and dependence on God, because God's kingdom comes through the Holy Spirit. So, no matter what we're doing, whether we're exercising our brains, praying or wiping someone's backside, we're looking to be energised by the Spirit. We are walking in the footsteps of Jesus.

This is what it looks like:

Matthew 7:16-20:

> *By their fruit you will recognise them. Do people pick grapes from thorn bushes, or figs from thistles? Likewise every good tree bears good fruit, but a bad tree bears bad fruit. A good tree cannot bear bad fruit, and a bad tree cannot bear good fruit. Every tree that does not bear good fruit is cut down and thrown into the fire. Thus, by their fruit you will recognise them.*

Galatians 5:16-24:

So I say, live by the Spirit, and you will not gratify the desires of the sinful nature. For the sinful nature desires what is contrary to the Spirit, and the Spirit what is contrary to the sinful nature. They are in conflict with each other, so that you do not do what you want. But if you are led by the Spirit, you are not under law.

The acts of the sinful nature are obvious: sexual immorality, impurity and debauchery; idolatry and witchcraft; hatred, discord, jealousy, fits of rage, selfish ambition, dissensions, factions and envy; drunkenness, orgies, and the like. I warn you, as I did before, that those who live like this will not inherit the kingdom of God.

But the fruit of the Spirit is love, joy, peace, patience, kindness, goodness, faithfulness, gentleness and self-control. Against such things there is no law. Those who belong to Christ Jesus have crucified the sinful nature with its passions and desires.

Matthew 25:–35-40:

[The King says]"'For I was hungry and you gave me something to eat, I was thirsty and you gave me something to drink, I was a stranger and you invited me in, I needed clothes and you clothed me, I was sick and you looked after me, I was in prison and you came to visit me.'

"Then the righteous will answer him, 'Lord, when did we see you hungry and feed you, or thirsty and give you something to drink? When did we see you a stranger and invite you in, or needing clothes and clothe you? When did we see you sick or in prison and go to visit you?'

> *"The King will reply, 'I tell you the truth, whatever you did for one of the least of these brothers of mine, you did for me.'"*

This section of the teaching of Jesus around judgment shows salvation is not something that can be earned, neither is it something that is based around being good. It suggests, however, that if the gift of salvation is authentic then the goodness will quite naturally be present. At times this might even be in spite of some theological systems, which fail to recognise the 'fruit' of care for the poor as the kite mark of genuine salvation. If Jesus is present through his Holy Spirit then these works of care and kindness will always be present in some form.

Reality

In any event, if you're doing something positive, even if you're not doing it for God but purely for selfish motives, it's better than doing either nothing or an evil thing, that's for sure. We are either part of the problem or part of the solution.

Many Christians do little other than critique and criticise and as such are perhaps unintentionally obstructing what God wants to do rather than flowing with it.

Ultimately, the finest measuring rod for everything we do is the life, teaching and person of Jesus Christ and all the revelation of Scripture as it flows towards him and out from him.

The message of Jesus is liberation. What happens in the physical realm will most certainly affect our spirit or inner core. The reverse is also true. The manifesto of Jesus brings his good news into every part of life and existence.

Many commentators including George Eldon Ladd observe that the kingdom of God is 'already but not yet', that it has come in part but is yet to arrive in its fullness. We live in the presence of the future, in the time of mixed motives and mixed experiences, so life is very messy and at times confusing. This means everything we do will be mixed both in motive and purity. Our experiences will also be bittersweet. This means we need to be humble when attempting to judge the efforts and attitudes of those around us. Furthermore, the world is a mixed place where the holy and the unholy, the perfect and the imperfect exist side by side. This will always be the case, that is until the end of the age (Matthew 13:24-30).

Messy Paradox

This good news, which represents liberation and freedom, is coming in stages and in different ways.

We had a crazy day about a month ago in our church. One individual was knocked off his bike and testified to God's miraculous protection and healing.

The same day, one of my friends was consoling a couple in hospital who had lost a baby after a full-term pregnancy.

How do you stack that up? It's the awesome pain of life, it's the power of evil and the nature of the human predicament. It's that God's kingdom has only come in part right now and it's about spiritual warfare. There's plenty of theology we could turn to and yet ultimately it's very difficult to make sense of any of this in the furnace of apparently random suffering.

On these occasions, only staying close to Jesus and open to God will see us through. We need to dig into God and hold on!

Jesus' message is about weeping with those who weep and mourning with those who mourn. It's about celebration, it's about feasting, it's about tasting the goodness of God. It's about fighting for his freedom, it's about an anger and a passion for justice.

As the Spirit of the Lord comes upon us, we're looking for release, we're looking for justice, we're looking to see God's power break out. We're desperate to see people find a relationship with Jesus and to be set free in the process, becoming more of who they're created to be. We want to see justice in the earth.

A friend of ours, Rachel Bentley, was a student in the 1980s and later went to work at the Body Shop as a researcher. Anita Roddick, who was the founder of the business with her husband Gordon, liked her and the fact that they had a shared passion for the poor, particularly children. This was the beginning of a long journey to the founding of a charity called Children on the Edge, which is still growing today.

Rachel is good friends with Maggie and one day they sat next to each other in a seminar when someone commented:

"We need to learn to release and repent of the anger that we feel."

Rachel turned to Margaret and said:

"Anger's the only thing that keeps me going! If I wasn't angry, I would do nothing!"

Rachel had learned to channel the anger she felt about the desperate plight of children around the world into her vocation, into her faith in God, and outwork it in action.

When Maggie was training as a psychosexual therapist before she set up Lifecentre, she went to work at a rape crisis centre that was run by survivors. None of them had any faith in God. Quite rightly, there was a lot of anger in the organisation.

After spending an evening on the phone counselling lines, the air turned blue on occasions when they went to the pub. Every request, sentence and conversation was filled with such hurt, anger, frustration, aggression and profanity! This anger was not positive. It kept wounds open, was projected onto the innocent and caused further pain and resentment. It needed to be purified and channelled.

Salvation and relationship with Jesus enables God's love and care to sift our anger.

God is the one who will ultimately judge, but it's very interesting to notice that after the extravagant celebrations of the wedding at Cana, the next thing Jesus did was arrive at the temple and start smashing it up (John 2:12-17)!

Here was a righteous anger, a "zeal" for the house of God, which consumed him. God is looking for a people whose lives are consumed by zeal for the message of Jesus Christ.

From invisible to visible

This zeal targets poverty, imprisonment, blindness and oppression. These things are both internal and external. They are emotional and physical.

It's about the person with panic attacks being released and set free. It's the community that is exploited and kept poor by unjust trade being liberated by the economics of fair trade.

These are all part of the same message, and when we look at the roots of Jesus' teaching in the book of Isaiah, we begin to realise that we spiritualise it at our peril.

Before you read further I would recommend you reading Isaiah 11:4, Isaiah 29:19, Isaiah 32:1 and Isaiah 32:7. Isaiah 58: 5-12 sums it up this way:

Is this the kind of fast I have chosen,
only a day for a man to humble himself?
Is it only for bowing one's head like a reed
and for lying on sackcloth and ashes?
Is that what you call a fast,
a day acceptable to the Lord?

Is not this the kind of fasting I have chosen:
to loose the chains of injustice
and untie the cords of the yoke,
to set the oppressed free
and break every yoke?

Is it not to share your food with the hungry
and to provide the poor wanderer with shelter—
when you see the naked, to clothe him,
and not to turn away from your own flesh and blood?

Then your light will break forth like the dawn,
and your healing will quickly appear;
then your righteousness will go before you,
and the glory of the Lord will be your rear guard.

Then you will call, and the Lord will answer;

you will cry for help, and he will say: Here am I.
"If you do away with the yoke of oppression,
with the pointing finger and malicious talk,

And if you spend yourselves in behalf of the hungry
and satisfy the needs of the oppressed,
then your light will rise in the darkness,
and your night will become like the noonday.

The Lord will guide you always;
he will satisfy your needs in a sun-scorched land
and will strengthen your frame.
You will be like a well-watered garden,
like a spring whose waters never fail.

Your people will rebuild the ancient ruins
and will raise up the age-old foundations;
you will be called repairer of broken walls,
restorer of streets with dwellings.

The currency of heaven

In his commentary, Alec Motyer observes that good news and justice are the currency of heaven. This begs the question: what is the currency of our churches, our expression of personal faith?

Is the currency of our faith good news, or is it something else?

I think it's such a relief that God is good. God is love and completely good in character, heart, in his dealings with us, in everything he promotes and in all he is.

In response to this I've written a simple liturgy. Now, I realise that this liturgy is not likely to pass the stringent tests of the

Church of England. But nevertheless, I've written it, and I would commend it to be shouted with great joy and laughter.

(Apologies to those who prefer the 1662!)

When I'm lost in darkness, what a relief!
(God is good!)
When I've blown it, what a relief!
(God is good!)
When my experience is dark and evil, what a relief!
(God is good!)
When I'm afraid, what a relief!
(God is good!)
When I expect the worst, what a relief!
(God is good!)
When I succeed, what a relief!
(God is good!)
When I'm happy and fulfilled, what a relief!
(God is good!)
Come rain or shine, what a relief!
(God is good!)

If we could just allow the truth that God is good and that he loves us to be embedded into our psyche, I think that would help us to reach out and be good news to others.

Alec Motyer also observes that good news means:

"Renewal and release from restrictions imposed by people that create the opposite of a harmonious society."

That's powerful. That's where the good news bites. There are restrictions in our world that cause breakdown, and the good news comes to break those down.

A friend of mine, Greg Valerio, has set up both a charity and a business called Cred. It's devoted to developing, sourcing and marketing fair trade silver and gold. He's also working more broadly in fair trade, which is about abolishing slavery and bringing social and economic liberation to communities long crushed and exploited by multi-national mining corporations. It's about bringing 'exodus' to whole tribes and even economic and social stability to entire nations.

In my mind, this is what the good news of the kingdom is about. It's about getting involved and beginning to see some change.

A year and a day

Jesus proclaims two things: a year and a day.

The Year of the Lord's favour connects with the year of Jubilee mentioned in the Old Testament. We'll look at this in more detail in a later chapter. It's a time of redistribution, sharing, a time of God's favour coming into the lives of all people to bring harmony and peace to all.

This is the age in which we're living. We are called to embody this year in our church communities, our families, our lifestyles and in our friendships. We want to live it out in every area of our lives.

But we also proclaim a day – a sudden arrival of judgment. This is 'too late time'.

The parable of the rich fool in Luke 12:20 shows that it can be too late. Inevitably, death comes and then eventually judgement.

So we are here to bring God's 'year' in the knowledge and the warning that the 'day' will come, and we should be thankful to God for his judgment. Thankful that Jesus Christ paid the price for our sin on the cross and that he took our judgement on himself (Colossians 2:13-15). Thankful that vengeance belongs to God and that all evil, be it individual or structural, will one day be judged by him (Romans 12:17-21).

When serial killer Harold Shipman died, people were phoning radio stations and the tone of their complaint was, "He's got away with it."

Well that's just not the case. There is a judgment.

Praise God that the books will be opened and somehow injustice will be put right. Praise God that our days are in the words of the psalmist, "like grass" (Psalm 103:15-16). We are in a season now where we can enjoy the love and justice of God, but we have a more beautiful day arriving when the kingdoms of this world become the kingdom of our Lord and of his Christ.

Why not take a pause to read Revelation 20:10 to Revelation 21:8?

Within the complex symbolism and imagery of this passage lies the assurance that evil will be destroyed and judgement will be brought. Ultimately, there can be no good, no love and no justice without judgement. The good news is not that we are not here to judge, but that we are to leave this to the God who is perfect. His judgement will be righteous, fair and final and will pave the way for the fullness of God's kingdom to fill the earth.

In the meantime, these words from Bishop John Sentamu sum up our responsibility:

> *Evangelism is all about good news: good news for the poor, freedom for prisoners, sight for the blind, release for the oppressed, all of which claim the sovereign reign of God in the world today. For too long the church has 'given up turf' and withdrawn to the safety of church life, failing to proclaim this good news with confidence and conviction. As a consequence, our society is like a building shored-up with scaffolding but lacking in firm foundations. The current task of the church is to reconnect imaginatively with the people of the twenty-first century. To do this, individual Christians need to communicate with confidence their own story of faith and understand how God's story still has the power to transform the lives of others in a similar way. Taking seriously Jesus' command to go and make disciples of all nations by word and deed.*

I remember one day arriving at Victoria train station in London. As I left the concourse I was anticipating a meeting over a rather nice lunch. However, I had a small amount of time, about fifteen minutes, and there was this guy on the side of the bus shelter shouting very seriously and in a menacing voice.

"Repent, or you will be damned, because God will judge you, because you are miserable filthy rotten sinners," he shouted.

Clearly here was a person with plenty of history and quite a few problems who was threatening people in the name of the good news.

I was initially aggravated by this, but he went too far when he began picking on a woman in the bus queue who had a young daughter.

"And as for you, allowing your daughter to listen to that filth [referring to a pop T-shirt she was wearing], and wear those clothes." [She looked quite trendy.]

Something clicked. I just thought, *"Fifteen minutes, ok that's enough."* So I stepped right in saying:

"Look here, dipstick! You are doing more damage to the gospel of Jesus than is imaginable! Why don't you get a therapist, get yourself a shrink?"

"Who are you, who are you, who do you think you are?" he retorted.

"Well," I said, "well, I'm a church pastor."

"You filthy heretic!" he interjected.

I thought, *"Well, that's not the first time I've been accused of that!"*

So I said: *"Look here, pal, get yourself some help. Get yourself in a community. Stop preaching this rubbish that's coming from inside you, and stop doing damage to the message of Jesus Christ."*

He looked at me and scuttled off.

Behind me the odd *"hear hear"* could be heard from the bus queue and even a couple of claps! I wish I could say that I then turned and shared the good news with the queue but I gathered myself, smiled at them and dashed off to my lunch.

This is an extreme example and I don't usually do that kind of thing. But we've got to ask, ultimately, are we good news or bad news? I believe that we are good news.

One aspect of Matthew 11:11-19 is the dichotomy between the Old Testament prophetic model and the New Testament prophetic model in Christ.

Jesus says:

> *"I tell you the truth: among those born of women there has not risen anyone greater than John the Baptist; yet he who is least in the kingdom of heaven is greater than he. From the days of John the Baptist until now, the kingdom of heaven has been forcefully advancing, and forceful men and women lay hold of it."*

And then he goes through and, in summary, says:

> *"Look, John came neither eating nor drinking and the religious said. 'Yes, that's demonic'. The Son of Man [Jesus] came eating and drinking and they say 'He's a glutton and a drunkard'."*

Here you see this contrast between the ministry of John, with his radical wilderness call and the kingdom ministry of Jesus, which was about going to parties, touching the untouchable, loving people, being generous and turning water into wine!

This was the cutting edge of his message. It's the whole heart of the Beatitudes (blessings) in Matthew 5. It's also behind his teaching on judgement (Matthew 7:1-5).

Ultimately, we don't come in judgment, we come alongside people as fellow travellers. The only difference between us as followers of Jesus and others is that we've been fortunate enough to meet him and be included in Christ.

Looking at Jesus in the New Testament causes us to radically re-examine ourselves. It's possible for us to be biblically non-Christian and that's what saddens me. Why is it that sometimes those who appear to believe the Bible can behave in such an inhuman manner? They continually appeal to Scripture but completely miss the message about having the heart of Jesus, who showed us what true humanity is like!

To those who lose the plot the message of Jesus is uncompromising:

Matthew 7:15-23 says:

> *"Watch out for false prophets. They come to you in sheep's clothing, but inwardly they are ferocious wolves. By their fruit you will recognise them. Do people pick grapes from thorn bushes, or figs from thistles? Likewise, every good tree bears good fruit, but a bad tree bears bad fruit. A good tree cannot bear bad fruit, and a bad tree cannot bear good fruit. Every tree that does not bear good fruit is cut down and thrown into the fire. Thus, by their fruit you will recognise them.*
>
> *"Not everyone who says to me, 'Lord, Lord,' will enter the kingdom of heaven, but only the one who does the will of my Father who is in heaven. Many will say to me on that day, 'Lord, Lord, did we not prophesy in your name and in your name drive out demons and in your name perform many miracles?' Then I will tell them plainly, 'I never knew you. Away from me, you evildoers!'"*

We need the Scriptures right at the heart of who we are. Jesus showed us how to step out. He touched and healed the woman with the flow of blood. He healed the paralytic on the Sabbath, breaking all the religious rules. He touched lepers.

Jesus went right to the edge. He broke down barriers. We have this wonderful message that is good news, and it really is so simple.

There are many grand theories, but it starts with just one person at a time.

So let's start where we are, doing the simple things, and allow God to open the way forward. Let's be prepared to break through some barriers and refuse to diminish the message of Christ by becoming unbalanced and preoccupied with only one aspect of the good news of Jesus.

POSTCARDS FROM MY FRIENDS
PAUL & PAULA WESTON

Paul and Paula are close friends of mine and I have visited them at New Generation Church in Sidcup many times. They are a wonderfully hospitable and loving community who have grown considerably over the last ten years. Their heart beats with the desire to be good news to their community and, as a result, they have some great stories of God's love breaking into people's lives. Here Paula tells just one of those stories. I have met the couple concerned and have seen firsthand what God has done for them.

Mary and Danny's Story

"Maybe I should do that Alpha course," remarked Danny, nodding towards the notice on the church snuggled among the houses in their little street.

"What would you want to do that for?" his partner Mary queried, with a hint of sarcasm in her voice.

A few months later, to her great surprise, Mary found herself agreeing to do a lunchtime Alpha with her friend. Regular attendees of the toddler group hosted by the church, Mary and the other mums had been invited to come along to Alpha.

By the end of the Alpha course Mary noticed changes: life didn't seem so hard any more. She wasn't so angry all the time and was happier at home.

At a Bible study a few months later, Mary gave her life to Jesus.

Danny and Mary had been together for fifteen years and Mary longed to get married.

They'd planned a wedding some years previously but the business they'd run together at the time had suddenly fallen apart and they found themselves in hard times. Mary had begun to grow bitter with her lot in life and moaned at Danny about their tatty little house and their lack of money. In fact, she moaned about a lot of things.

A few weeks after the Bible study Mary announced that she and Danny were getting married.

Danny had surprised her on the morning of her birthday; he'd even booked the registry office.

"What prompted Danny to sort it after all this time?" asked Mary's friends.

Mary said it was because she'd stopped moaning. Danny had asked her what she wanted for her birthday and instead of her annual response - a tirade of moans starting with how he couldn't afford anything anyway and look at the state of the house - Mary replied: "I don't need anything. I've got you and I've got the boys and I'm happy with that."

The wedding was on, a small service at the registry office and a reception to follow at Danny and Mary's house. Danny decided he would have to concrete their garden and erect a marquee to fit everyone in and even then it was going to be a squeeze.

Mary, who was yet to attend church on a Sunday or tell Danny about her newly found faith, had begun to go along each week to a small group with some mums from the church.

A few weeks after announcing their wedding plans, Mary was handed a card as she arrived at small group.

It was a gift from the church: a wedding reception including the venue and five-course meal with waitress service and all the trimmings.

Mary was overwhelmed and couldn't wait to tell Danny and the boys.

Danny and Mary were happily married just before Christmas.

The New Year arrived and Danny wanted Mary and the boys to join him on a trip to church on Sunday morning to say thank you to everyone for their wedding reception.

As Danny and Mary listened to the sermon they wondered if the people had known they were coming and if the preacher had written the sermon just for them. Based on the story of Ruth, everything that was said seemed to echo their own story.

They both knew God was speaking to them.

For the rest of the day, Mary and Danny talked and talked about their experience and what it all might mean.

They decided they must get to church every Sunday.

One morning Mary awoke to a lovely sunny day and flung back the curtains and surveyed the street.

Her eyes were drawn to an old lady's house across the street. She was a grumpy, tiresome old lady who didn't seem to want to be friends with any of her neighbours.

Mary had a strange feeling in the pit of her stomach and a thought popped into her head: 'Go and see if she's OK and if she needs anything'.

Mary busied herself with getting the boys ready for school, but she couldn't get the thought out of her head. So, with the boys safely in school, she knocked on her neighbour's door – ready for the rebuke to leave her alone.

However, as the door opened the elderly lady's eyes lit up and she looked expectantly at Mary.

"I've come to see if you're OK and if you need anything," faltered Mary.

"Who sent you?" came the quick reply.

"God sent me," said Mary.

"Who sent you?" the elderly lady asked again.

"God sent me."

The lady's face softened and she disclosed that the previous night, feeling so desperately alone, she had phoned the Samaritans, a Christian helpline, and now here was Mary standing on her doorstep.

Danny had begun to read the Bible and to talk to God as he worked.

When he heard a team from the church toddler group planned to go to Malawi he decided he wanted to be a part of the mission trip. He said he felt he had received so much that he wanted to give something back. In fact, he invited his nephew along too.

In Malawi, the rest of the team laughed lovingly at Danny's tear-stained face. Here was the man who had only ever cried twice in his adult life (at the births of his children), crying for what might have been the fifth time that day. After giving a pep talk to some of the team before they went into the orphanage, Danny found when they left that his tears were out of control. God was softening Danny's heart and was using the poor and needy, but beautiful, children of Malawi to do it.

The family was now attending church regularly and Danny's work, which had been slack for a long time, picked up. Danny, finding himself much busier and realising that this was God's blessing on them, decided to give the blessing away and employ his nephew, mainly to get him out of a difficult situation that wasn't at all helpful to him.

Although work was now flowing in, debts that had built up didn't seem to be clearing and Danny returned from Malawi to find a letter demanding the repossession of their house unless several thousand pounds were found by the end of the month.

Mary was at her wits end and, fearing the loss of their home, was overwhelmed by despair. In her disappointment she turned against God. As Danny urged her to come to church she reluctantly agreed but said this would be the last time she would walk through those doors. God was prepared and the message Mary heard that morning yet again felt as if it was specifically for her. She said sorry to God and softened her heart towards him once again.

Mary confided in one of the mums in her cell group, telling her of the impending repossession and consequent struggle with God. As Mary left for home, the mum sent a quick text to a few of Danny and Mary's friends in the church and by the end of the week an envelope dropped through Danny and Mary's door. Coming from a few anonymous church friends, that envelope containing the exact amount of money they needed to pay the mortgage company.

Almost a year after being blessed with a wedding reception by the church, Danny realised it was time to give in to God. He committed his life to God and was baptised that same day.

Mary had been baptised a few months earlier and their walk with Jesus continues to grow.

CHAPTER 3:
PEOPLE

We have now just begun to peel back the layers of this passage, revealing the beauty of the heart and passion of God. It really is a relief to find that our Saviour is both so glorious and human. The God we worship is the fullest expression of love, goodness and justice. His message is truly *the* good news.

Luke 4:17-21 and Isaiah 61:1-2 link together. In Luke 4, Jesus is proclaiming and fulfilling Isaiah 61. In his life and ministry he both interprets and contextualises it.

Before we go on, take some time to read it slowly, one verse at a time, taking five minutes to pause at the end of each verse to ask God to speak to you. As you do so, take some time to thank him in your own words for all you see as you reflect on each verse.

Luke 4:17-21:

> *The scroll of the prophet Isaiah was handed to him. Unrolling it, he found the place where it is written:*
>
> *"The Spirit of the Lord is on me, because he has anointed me to preach good news to the poor.*
> *He has sent me to proclaim freedom for the prisoners*

and recovery of sight for the blind,
to release the oppressed, to proclaim the year of the Lord's favour."

Then he rolled up the scroll, gave it back to the attendant and sat down. The eyes of everyone in the synagogue were fastened on him, and he began by saying to them, "Today, this Scripture is fulfilled in your hearing."

So far we have observed that this message is the kerygma – it's the essence. It contains the essence of who Jesus is, of his message, of why he came.

When Jesus read, "The Spirit of the Lord is upon me", or in the words of Isaiah 61. "The Spirit of the sovereign Lord is upon me", he was expressing his identity as the 'one', the Messiah. At the same time he's paving the way for us, the Church of God, to follow in his footsteps. We can also be anointed by the Spirit of God.

This Spirit is both attracted by, and present within, every expression of God's goodness and purposes. There are instances in the Scriptures of God anointing those who are clearly not committed to him (Cyrus the dictator in Isaiah 44:28 and 45:1 and Balaam's donkey in Numbers 22:28).

In the New Testament we see men and women positioned by God miraculously to be used by him (the Ethiopian eunuch in Acts 8:26-40). It seems reasonable to conclude that while God likes to work through his people, the Church, that his Spirit is also incredibly active in sustaining, filling and influencing the whole of creation.

In that process he is also using all kinds of people who are ready and available as his agents in many different situations, even if they have not yet to come to faith in Christ. Hence, many of those who immerse themselves in causes that are close to the heart of God without knowing Jesus are *"not far from the kingdom of God"* (Mark 12:33-34).

All the activity of God's kingdom in the earth is energised by the Holy Spirit. If we want to get things done, we need to get ourselves filled, zapped, soaked or whatever term makes most sense bearing in mind our Christian backgrounds (or baggage)! In short, we need to encounter God's Spirit.

Lastly, we have seen that God is good and that his message is good news. This good news encapsulates not just what we believe and say, it should characterise who we are and how we live. It's about a spiritual realm that embraces the whole of creation and existence, be it the visible or invisible.

In this chapter we will explore the personal and individual thread that weaves its way through the manifesto. Next we're going to look at the transformation of society, looking at the big picture. But before rushing on I want to take time to reflect on how focused and passionate God is about every individual human being.

When Christ came to the earth, he laid his life down for every individual human being that had already lived and would be born in the future. It's a very, very simple point, but it's one that can become as familiar as the dawn. We can take it for granted. How often do we take time to experience and marvel at the beauty of each day as it dawns? Yet we enjoy the consequences of the dawn each day as light rises, the sun warms the earth and photosynthesis begins again, causing everything to grow and flourish.

Similarly, the day of the kingdom of God has dawned. It has not yet run its full course, but we are living in the light, warmth and productivity of salvation. Let's rejoice in this and make the most of it.

If we are to be true to the values of Christ we must share his passion for people and his desire to meet each individual right where they are.

People or structures?

At one level, models of 'Church' – while being important – should never be central. We may ask, "Is the Church an institution, or is it an organisation?" Most of us will make a choice as to where we fit and what we believe.

My own conviction is that there is no normative pattern for church in Scripture, but some very important frameworks are revealed. Without doubt, the apostle Paul's favourite analogy for church was the body. It's a relational model, one that gives emphasis to each individual as well as to the whole. Each person, with his or her unique gifts and contributions, has a valuable place in the whole community of faith.

So, whatever else the Church is about, whatever the Church looks like, however it's formed and structured, right at its core is its people. The Church that lives authentically for the message of the good news of the kingdom will be people-centred. People will take precedence above tradition, programmes, mission or whatever the presenting vision might be.

Why is it that we often meet loads of people who think, "Jesus is cool, I kind of like Jesus, he's brilliant. But the Church leaves me cold?"

There's no easy answer to this, but one reason I see is that many Christians have lost their passion for people. We need to grow our connections to our communities and to different people groups. We need to connect with the heart of people, right where they are, because that's what God's heart is about. Talk to a new person with regard to their initial impressions of any church and their feedback will most likely revolve around their sense of welcome and relational connection rather than the quality of the sermon or the 'correctness' of the mode of church.

We are called to be specialists in love, forgiveness and acceptance. We should be enthusiastic learners in holding parties, expressing family life and enjoying relationships that breathe hope, healing and life. This makes church members refreshing to be around, just like Jesus.

After all, 5,000 people marched into the wilderness after him without so much as a packed lunch! He must have been pretty fabulous to be around.

Looking back at Isaiah 58, we see it's part of these prophesies Jesus was fulfilling. Verses six and seven are very well known verses that talk about prayer, fasting and worship.

Isaiah 58:6-8:

> *Is not this the kind of fasting I have chosen:*
> *to loose the chains of injustice*
> *and untie the cords of the yoke,*
> *to set the oppressed free*
> *and to break every yoke?*
> *Is it not to share your food with the hungry*
> *and to provide the poor wanderer with shelter –*

when you see the naked, to clothe him,
and not to turn away from your own flesh and blood?
Then your light will break forth like the dawn…

Perhaps it's easier for us to have this great vision of a just society and to pray passionately for it. But the million-dollar questions are: how does this happen? How can this be? How can we change a society?

A few years ago the Bible Society had a wonderful strapline for one of its campaigns: *"Changing the world, one person at a time"*.

This is how things change, and one of the core threads of this passage relates to people and relationships. It's all about people, it's all about individuals. This is great news for some of us because we know we are not particularly strategic, that we are never going to be 'super saints'. We don't really know what we are doing. We are just living in the moment.

My daughter Chloe is like that. By this I mean she shares much in common with our flat-coated Labrador. They have remarkably similar personalities as they are both very people-centred and affectionate.

Chloe loves the presence of the Holy Spirit but is very people-focused. Every one of her school reports had the same theme: "Chloe just needs to spend more time on her studies and less time looking after all the other people around her. She needs to focus on her work and care less about others."

This gave us a moral dilemma as Christian parents. Do we try and get her to focus on her studies more (not a bad outcome in itself) and at the same time care less for others?

We knew as parents that there's something of the heart and the passion of God that is firing her heart for people.

Isaiah 58:7 talks about food, shelter and clothing. That requires personal involvement. People are not just issues; we are challenged about bringing the issue home.

In the early days of our marriage, Maggie was a teacher. Being fresh out of college helped her connect with some of the pupils, and morning by morning two of them would turn up with a girl who, at the age of fourteen, was already a borderline alcoholic.

They'd bring her to the classroom drunk and Maggie would sneak her to the back cupboard in the classroom, ply her with black coffee and talk to her. Over a period of time, it became clear she was being systematically abused at home. It was a very difficult situation and seemed impossible to unravel. She ended up living in our home. This brought the issue right into our hearts, which was very formative for all of us.

We became very close to her and shared a deep family link, which was quite explosive at times. In these moments my lack of pastoral sensitivity was severely stretched. One night I went into her room and there was an empty bottle of vodka with razor blades all lined up. She already had scars on her arm and there she was ready to cut herself. I said "What do you think you're *** doing?" in an angry and reactive manner. She said "I'm gonna **** cut myself so **** off."

Maggie appeared at the door, at which stage the girl shot outside the house and sat outside in her car. Maggie sarcastically exclaimed, "Well done!" followed by ironic clapping. I had not been particularly smart, particularly bearing in mind she'd previously tried to kill herself by crashing her car!

Maggie went out to the car, in the dark and freezing cold, and gently started to talk to her through the car window. Eventually she responded saying: "I'll come in as long as he's not there when I come in!" So there I am hiding in my own home, cowering behind the stairs, ready to give her a humble apology. We learned so much by having this lovely person in our home.

She became very close to our hearts, an important part of our family and a wonderful friend to our kids. More than twenty years later, she is still part of our lives, even though she lives and works in another part of the country.

This was the beginning of a journey for us. She was a beautiful person who was loved and called by God, who needed us to be his hands and arms. We realised that we can talk about noble principles but if we're not willing to let people invade our hearts and our lives, capturing our affection and taking our time, then we are not even 'at the races'.

We're in danger of becoming nothing more than good, green, eco-principled, middle-class, fair-trade-tea-sipping Christians!

We could be a lot worse I guess, although I'm convinced that most flavoured tea emanates from the dark side! Strawberry tea? It's not right! I like my tea good and English (although of course no tea really is). I'm sure there's something perverse about flavoured tea, although my wife will testify otherwise.

In any case, the gospel is all about bringing the issue home. Let's not just be full of principles, even values; let's touch people's lives and let them touch ours. Let's lose our hearts knowing that they will most likely be bruised and broken, but that at least we will be close to the heart of God.

I often imagine how I would feel if my son or daughter was ravaged, trapped or captured by poverty, injustice, sexual violence or any other major struggle. I would be heartbroken. Imagine how God feels about every human being! We should not feel that he is unable to support and sustain us bearing in mind he stays so perfectly whole, good and full of fun, hope and glory, while at the same time carrying such continual suffering and pain.

Let's journey together and be enriched, learning as much about ourselves as we do about others as we serve them.

Both Isaiah 61:1 and Luke 4:18 talk about the "oppressed". What does that mean?

Literally, the word here means *"all those who are broken by life"*.

Jesus came and proclaimed good news, release and freedom from oppression. Literally, to all those who've been broken by life. This covers every class, race, nation and economic and social background. It covers relational rejection, abuse from others, all addictions and any other oppression that could be named.

Jesus comes and breaks the chains, and the same Spirit that was on Jesus is upon us. We are in the chain-breaking business. That is what we are here for. The great news is that God doesn't just deal with the issues, he brings back what's been lost. He restores and redeems. That's what is so wonderful.

It's great fun being married to a psychosexual therapist. Every now and then you get to talk to some people that Maggie and her team have helped. I was talking to one couple and the great news is that when the woman returned from psychosexual therapy feeling that a lot of her past issues had been dealt with, she found her sexual desire had been restored. To their delight they got their sex life back. This caused the husband to ponder the fact that there might be a God after all!

That's good news for both the husband and the wife, as well as for all those around them who don't know what's been going on but have a stake in their relationship. Children benefit from having parents who are more in love and are creating a home full of joy. Parents become less worried about the marriages of their offspring. Friends and work colleagues get to hang out and work with people who are less uptight and frustrated!

Now that's what the kingdom is about. This kingdom of God is not an ethereal realm that's 'out there'. It breaks tangibly into the earth as God gets involved in every place where he is welcomed. We've heard that the only truly secular thing is sin - well this gospel of the kingdom breaks into the whole of life, giving us a new future.

I sat with a young guy a while ago. He shared with me:

"My marriage was terrible for five years. We had five years of hell, five years of resentment and distance. Much of it was my fault – I was insensitive, I was too focused on my career, and my wife and family suffered."

I said, "What changed for you?"

He said, "Well, years ago I said sorry to my wife. I'd tried everything, but she could not forgive me. After five years, suddenly one day, she had a revelation from God that because Jesus had forgiven her, maybe she could forgive me, and that changed everything. From that moment on, our whole marriage turned around."

That's the process. There's no fixed pattern. But when God comes, he meets us personally. So our focus needs to be intensely individual and personal; because God is a relational God.

All of the outward trappings of faith such as values, doctrines, creeds, behaviours and frameworks, are like clothes wrapped around a God who is love and has humanity in his heart.

This knowledge and experience should be enough to cure the constipation of religion. It should be enough for us that he has us in his heart. If we know we are loved by God we can love ourselves. We are then freed to love others.

The person behind the issue

We are all able to look at people differently when we know their story. Maggie and I went out for a meal with some friends who we really like. After a lovely meal over three courses and a couple of glasses of wine we were sitting in their lounge chilling out. I'm starting to get 'the look' from across the room. Any husband will know this situation. If I try to give my wife a 'look' she never has a clue what I'm on about. However, all I need is one look to know she's thinking, "Get me home – I'm tired!"

I know that I ignore this at my peril, as I would normally get a telling off on the way home in the car. But on this occasion I decided we'd better go home and was just about to make the move when the wife of the other couple leaned forward intently and with great sincerity exclaimed:

"Now, about homosexuality…"

I thought, *"Oh, dear Jesus… help me!"*

She said, *"Now, I'm very worried."*

"Well what are you worried about?" I replied.

"Well, you know, there've been some conversations at one of the men's groups, and it's come to my attention that a number of gay couples have started attending our meetings. What do you think about that?"

I felt like saying, *"Well, short of running around the centre of Chichester in my underwear shouting, 'Hallelujah', I can't think of much else to do or say!"*

However, instead I asked: *"Are you confident that I'm not about to sway away from the heart of Jesus or the orthodox biblical view of sex and sexuality?"*

"Yes," she replied.

"So what are you worried about?"

"I don't know. I'm just afraid of what it might mean."

So I said, *"Let me tell you a story."* And this is what I told her.

"There was a young girl who was sexually abused throughout her childhood and into her early teenage years. She had an encounter with Christ but she went through terrible struggles and problems with self-harming and other issues.

"She began to step out into the workplace a little and started to work with people who had come from similar backgrounds. She met a young man and they got together. He beat and abused her, treating her terribly. She came out the end of that relationship completely broken.

"At this stage, when she was in a mess, she met another woman, formed a friendship with her and ended up in an exclusive relationship with her. She stopped self-harming and the love and security of the friendship eradicated her suicidal urges. She's been promoted through her job. She's stable in her life. She's happy and fulfilled. Now, what do you say about that?"

The husband looked at me dumbfounded.

"Look, I'm not saying this is tidy, that it's perfect, but they're on a journey. I'm not saying this is the end. I'm not saying it's not complicated. But believe me, we've got a church full of people whose lives aren't ideal. We've got a church full of people who are struggling to make their lives make sense and to grow closer to God. What they need is grace, love and space. How do you feel now?"

He said: *"Do you know, I kind of feel differently, because now I see that behind every label there's a person and behind every person there's a story. And when you know the story it's easier to understand and accept the person and forget the label."*

For most gay people, chosen or experienced gay orientation has nothing to do with traumatic experience. I share this story to illustrate that behind issue, whether it's homelessness, sexuality, addiction, anger or selfishness, there's a person who has his or her own unique story. We are all who we are at least in part as a result of our life experiences.

This doesn't mean to say in any way that we step aside from what we believe at the macro level or that we neglect God's ideal. However, I think when we connect with people we suddenly realise that God doesn't see gays or straights - he just sees people who are precious in his sight.

The incarnation of Jesus not only shows us what God is like, but also what it's like to be truly human. We look to Jesus, he is our goal. The good news is that the dark pictures we see of humanity in the news are not the whole truth. Let's not be overwhelmed. Let's not be afraid to reach out.

Jesus stepped across the line time and time again to reach people who were alienated from God. This God wants to make us more like Jesus. More fully human, more able to love and connect.

It's sin that animalises us. It's sin that depersonalises us. Sometimes when we slip up we say, "Well, I'm only human". Well that's no excuse because Jesus was the fullest expression of God's intention for humanity. He should be our goal and it's his death on the cross that opens the door for the cleansing and forgiveness of God, enabling us to aspire to greater things.

What are you involved in that needs to stop? Maybe no-one else knows about it... Do you feel crushed by things that have taken place? The good news is you can draw a line under these things and not let them define who you are.

People as objects

One of the greatest sins in our society is the treatment of people as objects or issues rather than individuals who have a unique story full of pains and passions. Once you know somebody's story it's so much easier to connect with them.

Maybe you've been treated as a commodity, or you've treated others this way. Well, the love of God the Father changes everything.

The story in the first three chapters of Genesis says so much about both humanity and God. I love the picture of God walking in the garden, looking for Adam and saying, "Adam, where are you?" (Genesis 3:8-9.)

What is this about? Has the God who created the universe suddenly become a little absent-minded? "Now where's Adam - I seem to have mislaid him!"

I don't think so. He knew where Adam was, he just wanted Adam to be aware of what had happened to him and what trouble he was in as a result.

God seeks out each person one by one, by name. You are not a number. God knows you by name.

I think we've got to be careful in our churches with regard to the kind of culture we create. I'm all for systems, structures and frameworks where they serve people. We want to care for people well. People deserve the best care we can possibly give and the best love we could possibly give. The bigger we get as churches, the more structures we need to have in place to facilitate this.

However, I sometimes get depressed when I hear leaders speak. It's all about targets, goals, projects or the institution.

Preoccupation with traditional practices, numbers and success at the expense of people will have dire consequences. It's not about numbers, it's about people. Any church that loses this focus is vulnerable to missing the heart of God.

All leaders of organisations involving people need supervision or mentoring. We need input. We need to get a life! We need to go fishing! Because when we're leading people, our care and compassion can be eroded. Often when people come to a church they begin to feel safe. So when they go through pain and agony, they look for the best place to outwork that pain safely and that's often the church.

So they come and kick the living daylights out of the pastor (metaphorically speaking) or anybody who's around them. Wonderful! It often feels like a dubious privilege to be the recipients of the pain of others as they sound off. The only comfort we can find is in thanking God that these people feel safe enough to behave badly and let out some of their feelings. Sometimes people's bad behaviour can be a compliment.

Life as a leader in the workplace is often the same. It can feel a lonely place at times. That's why we need to keep ourselves fresh as human beings so we do not lose our heart of compassion and become hardened.

We need to keep our marriages fresh. We need to enjoy life. We need to taste the coffee, we need to smell the roses and keep ourselves whole and grounded so we can be energised to be like Jesus for people.

Gerald Coates often says: *"Basically, God doesn't want churches that operate like a clock: tick-tock, tick-tock, tick-tock – a perfectly even and mechanistic system. He wants churches that have a heartbeat which, while it moves with a rhythm, has a more irregular, human and organic pattern."*

These types of churches are a bit irregular and a bit messy, but under the surface there's a heart that beats.

Gerald goes further and states: *"God wants us to have churches where people feel free to sin!"* You can imagine a somewhat angry or bemused reaction in many settings.

He's not promoting sin but expressing a heartfelt longing for churches where people can be honest and real. So let's put away pious platitudes and realise the good news is about people with all their real experiences. It's about the things that are important to people. Love, sex, relationships, acceptance, ambition and the future. All of these are spiritual issues from God's perspective.

We should seek to create churches where people can be open, feel safe and learn to live with the tensions that this creates.

I love what GK Chesterton said: *"Humanity is both the glory and the rubbish of the universe."*

We touch the depravity that's around us but we mustn't get consumed by it.

Jim McNeish often says: *"Perception without love is a sin."*

Oh boy, am I in trouble! How many times do we perceive with judgement, selfishness, self-righteousness or impatience? Yet perception without love is a sin.

All the evaluation, theology, sociology, science and truth is ultimately sinful if not carried through the lens of love, and love is rooted in relationships.

Sometimes as we live and work in such a broken world we can wonder whether anything's changing. However, it's all about 'one person at a time'. The kingdom of God comes one person at a time. Renewal and revival come one person at a time. Justice and peace come one life, one family, one community and ultimately one nation at a time.

God's kingdom involves this incredible mixture of healing, deliverance and prayer with people's lives being dramatically transformed.

If you took the miracles out of the four gospels and the book of Acts, you would end up with one or two bits of teaching and a few meals! So much of it is miraculous that we must appreciate this is part of who God is and how he wants to work in us.

However, it's also about God's provision through restored relationships and community, which is built around the core teaching of Jesus Christ. This is part of the miracle, it's part of human wellbeing. It's about relationships and family.

A while ago a young guy aged nineteen came to me and said: "*Roger, I need a father figure*". I responded to him: "*Look Fred* [his name wasn't really Fred], *I'm not sure that I can aspire to that great and noble goal.*"

His father had left home when he was fourteen and, despite the best efforts of an excellent mother, Fred needed some male input. He had no plans or strategy, no-one to kick him helpfully up the backside or speak directly when he needed it. So I said, "*I can fulfil that role for you!*"

We sat down together and talked, and it transpired that he was going round in circles educationally. We talked and prayed about plans for his life. We talked about the call of God upon his life. We talked about his passion for Jesus and we continued to meet bi-weekly to keep in touch. Two or three years later he actually managed, much to his surprise, to get into university. He's come out the other end with straight A grades!

Can I take the credit? Absolutely not. All the hard work was his. But I was there to believe in him, encourage him and prod him when he needed it.

This is what the Church is all about. We're living through the tensions. We're battling for people's freedom and wholeness. We're standing with them. We will sink or swim with them. At times we will see them delivered from the fire and on other occasions they will be in the fire. No matter what we will stand with them as people.

Felt needs

Isaiah 61:1 talks about Jesus coming to bind up and to bandage. This carries a sense of personal attention, soothing, healing and restoring to wholeness.

To do this we must understand the 'felt needs' and learn to discern these in people. To do this we need to meet them, hear them, hang out with them, include them and get to know them.

The whole area of the broken heart also comes out in Isaiah 61. This covers any and every human breakdown; emotional brokenness, depression and breakdown through the damaging things we've done to ourselves and others. This includes anything that has entangled and chained us up. These things come together in this message and define our agenda: to see the chains broken.

I love it in James 5:16 where it says: *"Confess your sins to one another and you will be healed."*

We're here to hear people's confession, to pray and to release them in the name of Jesus. Ninety percent of the members of our church are in small community groups (cells), which meet in homes week by week. In ours we make room for everyone to tell their life stories using dialogue, music, creativity or just by telling the story.

These have been times of great emotion and shock. I could swear that on one occasion I saw the wallpaper rolling up the wall in reaction to the painful honesty! People were unlocking secrets that had never been told, marriages were being strengthened, people were being reconciled to parents and lost children, drawn out of depression, encouraged to go for great things and to keep going.

We've learned that we need to create a loving connection in Jesus in which there's a level of safety that enables us to really journey together. Because spirituality is about both vertical and horizontal relationships, relationship between us and God and also between us and other human beings. We can't say we love God if we hate other people (1 John 2:9-10). Our wholeness or the dysfunction in our relationships with God will be mirrored in our relationships with people, and vice versa.

As a 'kingdom community', church will be messy, full of the impure as well as the pure gold because we can only be ourselves. There will be sinners and imperfect people who are on a journey with God. This journey cannot be travelled alone and should be embarked upon with many different companions. Some help us and we may be able to help others. In reality the process of giving is as healthy and life-giving as receiving.

This passage gives us faith for what is possible. We can be confident that as we meet people and as we touch their lives, God has given us the tools in Christ that enable a little bit of heaven to break in to any situation.

At the Lifecentre building, where many come to share their deepest, darkest and most painful experiences of hurt and abuse, there is a long entrance corridor. On the walls a local artist has painted a stunning mural of caterpillars going through the metamorphosis into beautiful butterflies. Underneath are the words:

"Just when the caterpillar thought its life was over, it turned into a butterfly."

That, in essence, is the message of the good news of Jesus to every individual. It's relevant to every life experience now but also supremely relevant to life after death.

Death is not the end. Through the death and resurrection of Jesus Christ, eternity is opened to us. However, eternal life can be tasted now. God's power is available for all of us. Jesus was people-centred. More than that, he crossed the line to meet people where they were at. Time and time again, Jesus reached out to people, he crossed boundaries. God is calling us as churches to cross the line; to meet people exactly where they are.

In Luke 19:1-9 we see Zacchaeus the tax collector, who is universally despised. He's a pariah, someone who's rejected and hated by his community because he has colluded with their Roman oppressors. Jesus goes to eat with him. He crossed the line.

In Mark 10: 46-52 we see Bartimaeus, the blind man, who's sitting by the roadside begging. Jesus is walking past. He's shouting out. Everybody's saying *"Shut up, shut up!"* Jesus comes back and has the love and the dignity to treat him as a human being and say, *"What is it you want?"*

Mary, the woman who had led an immoral life, washed Jesus' feet with her tears and dried them with her hair (John 12:1-8). The other religious leaders were scandalised and would have sat in judgement. By contrast, Jesus received her act of love.

Again we see with the woman caught in adultery in John 8:1-11 and the Samaritan woman at the well in John 4:1-26 that Jesus crossed the line. He crossed racial barriers, barriers of sex and gender and religious barriers in order to connect with people and to share the love of God in the moment. Through these events we see the Holy Spirit breaking out and doing what he does best: meeting people and seeing them change.

Sometimes Christians talk a great deal about their 'positions', both in terms of theology and practice. Well, it seems that God's position is that he loves people and he's laid down his life for us so that we might know him!

This leaves us with the question: "Where can I cross the line and begin meeting people where they are?'

This is what Jesus did time and time again, he broke out and he connected with people. This is a consequence and fulfilment of Jesus' wonderful manifesto.

I will leave the final words to some of the people who have visited Lifecentre:

"I feel I have been able to overcome so much by coming to Lifecentre, it has been good to let it all out and be able to look at my

feelings. What's been so good is that I can leave it all behind because I trust Lifecentre. It is a safe place and really friendly. I can now be a little girl and not a grown up." **Girl aged 11.**

A boy aged 10 *abused in a paedophile ring wrote his counsellor a card saying: "You are a good listener, you have helped me a lot, you are making me more confident. Thank you."*

A girl aged 14 said: *"Coming to counselling gives me a place to be believed and listened to, and you like me. I feel no-one else really likes me, but you do."*

"I feel I have gained the ability to share and explore the forbidden secret insight into my relations. I now do not feel shame and guilt as it was not my fault. Everyone at Lifecentre has been very friendly and welcoming, which I appreciated." **Man in his sixties.**

"I feel I have gained the ability to deal with my flashbacks and have more confidence to move on as I now know it wasn't my fault. My counsellor has been easy to talk to as Lifecentre is a safe place." **Boy aged 14.**

"After I was attacked all of my relationships broke down. I was humiliated, living in fear, scared to go out. I was spending all my time at home crying with the curtains closed and doors locked. On my twenty-second birthday I took steps to end my own life. Somehow I survived. I realised I needed help. Since Lifecentre, I am able to go out. I'm slowly starting to get my confidence back. I don't get as many bad dreams or sleep with a baseball bat under my pillows. I can laugh now and six weeks ago I wore a dress. **Woman aged 22.**

POSTCARDS FROM MY FRIENDS
SYLVIA MAY

Sylvia and Leo May are two of our close friends. We have holidayed together. Maggie and Sylvia while away many an hour talking to one another on their mobile phones. Sylvia leads our cell group at Revelation Church and her full-on openness is what has helped us grow together. Here's a little of her story:

We all have different ways of dealing with stress, mine was to eat.

No, this wasn't comfort eating with lovely homemade, slightly too rich or sweet food. This was secret eating, whereby you shove any food into your mouth. Well maybe not quite any, as ideally there would always be a high salt, sugar or fat element. A bag of apples wouldn't have done the trick. But it was always, always in secret.

In retrospect I can see that it started as early as six years old. I found that the only way to block the pain caused by the bad things that were happening to me was to eat, eat and eat until I could almost burst.

Of course, the only way to get away with eating that volume of food was to steal it from the larder, fridge or freezer (yes, and not even wait for it to be defrosted) or spend every penny of my pocket money on it.

I didn't allow myself to think about what I was doing as it was only in the early stages, maybe a once or twice a week occurrence, but it made me an expert secret keeper. By the time I was ten the secrets had become more numerous.

When I went to boarding school for a very brief spell it dawned on me that I truly did have a problem. My tuck box full of sweets, chocolates and crisps, which was supposed to last me until half term, was devoured under my bedcovers in one night. The rest of the term was hell, though I managed to steal puddings and biscuits during some of the meals.

No-one knew, no-one even guessed what pain I was in. It was just another secret.

From the outside, I looked like quite a happy, confident child, who thankfully was blessed with a fairly attractive demeanour, which meant I could get away with ever-increasing hips and thighs. I hated them, but it was easier to hate them than hate those that had done bad things to me, and most of all those who had let me down.

If only I could have cried and screamed, ranted and raved, but it was easier to just go into my secret world of eating whenever the pain got too much.

By the time I was 16, I had left school and was living and working in the south of France by myself. It's too long a story to explain, but suffice to say that as a teenager with long blonde hair I was ripe for getting into stuff well beyond my capabilities, many of which were also dangerous. More bad things happened and, as they did, I resorted more to secret eating. By this stage I was a very voluptuous girl, which again caused other bad experiences to come my way.

I was trapped; trapped in a world of secrets and darkness.

At those times I felt a million miles from God but, looking back, I see how close he must have been to me as I can't think how else I would have survived. I did know of him as I had been brought up going to church every week, and I even went sometimes in Nice.

However, my faith was very limited. It was a one-way street, with me doing none of the listening. I just couldn't hear God and church was really a habit, something you did on a Sunday morning. It was a time to mix with nice people, who seemingly had no secrets as dark as mine; a time to forget.

Coming back to Central London four years later threw me into more of the same. More bad things happened and I felt trapped in seemingly endless cycles of pain with no relief. This was clearly my destiny, to be the keeper of secrets.

My first marriage was to a man of no faith, which was mistake number one. Mistake number two was being totally naive and blind to what I was getting myself into, but then again I would have married the first man that asked me. It was nice to be asked anything as I had got so used to people just taking. He had huge debts, which I found out about on day two of our supposed honeymoon, which got cancelled when the VAT man arrived at our door!

I spent the eighties, which for most people were the heydays, sunk in a loveless, debt-ridden marriage. Although my husband was kind, he was also massively controlling. He didn't want me to work, which left me agoraphobic, except for when I crept out to get my stash of food when he wasn't around. When the debt dragged on after five years I had to go out to work, which was my saving grace.

I was interviewed by a man who, only seeing my facade, thought I was the bee's knees, and for the first time in my life I had someone who believed in me. He saw my abilities, the real Sylvia, rather than the voluptuous blonde. I was hooked, and for the first time in my life I soared like an eagle, weight dropping off me; I was happy, confident and proud of myself.

The secrets were still there, but the compulsive eating had stopped.

I left my husband, which burdened me with more guilt. They say guilt is a wasted emotion, but how do you lose it? I later found out that only Christ could help me there. At the time I had not been to church for years.

Ten years of success followed in London. I had great jobs, a great social life and a little church, though again, much like my early years, I felt no closeness to God.

I married again and due to my firstborn being ill, decided to give up my highly paid job and move back to Chichester, where I had spent my childhood years. Another son followed.

The death of my brother (aged 40) triggered my old eating habits and the memory of my many secrets. The nightmare started again.

A dark period in my marriage followed. Suffice to say I was weighed down by the fact that it felt like every man or woman I had met in my forty-five years had let me down. I felt it was the end and I contemplated suicide. Food became the escape again and now there were even more secrets.

The suicide of my cousin drove me to the edge and shortly after a run along the beach one morning I heard God for the first time telling me to go to church.

It had been on my mind for a while, so I had looked at a few in the area to go and visit. Imagine my amazement when on returning home that very morning I received a call from Revelation inviting me to take part in an Alpha course.

I walked into church that Sunday and all I can say is that I knew I had come home, home into the arms of my heavenly Father, the one who had never let me go and had never let me down.

I cried every Sunday for months as the Holy Spirit washed over me, and I heard God constantly after that, directing and guiding all my moves.

The Lifecentre, through counselling, helped me so much and I was able to unload all my secrets, even those I had been unable to tell my husband about.

My baptism (carried out by Roger) was on the day of my cousin's memorial. I don't believe that was a coincidence, it was God's way of saying to me that, through the death of Jesus, I was reborn – and I was.

Life took on a fresh complexion, with God restoring and healing so many areas. Through various channels, such as the marriage course, counselling and good Christian friends, my marriage started to be rebuilt brick by brick.

In some ways, however painful those periods were, my marriage is now the richer for all we have learned together and we hope that we can use our pain to help others in the future.

Nothing is ever as transparent and as straightforward as it seems, certainly in marriage with all the complexities it throws up. So we hope to show people, through personal testimony, that no matter how dire situations feel sometimes, God can and does restore. Love is very powerful.

I started to lead a church cell group, which felt unbelievably empowering. Little me being trusted to be part of what I truly feel is God's work in leading a church home group. More prayer and personal testimonies from different members of the group led to the Holy Spirit being tangibly present in our meetings.

At this time I worked part-time looking after my cousin, who was fifty but had a mental age of eight. She had Down's syndrome and was living partly independently, but not very well. I would bathe her, take her food shopping and have some one-on-one time with her.

Driving back one day from such a shopping trip, it occurred to me that I had never prayed with her before. How ridiculous was that? I asked her if she would like me to pray for her and she nodded and indicated that she wanted me to hold her hand. I prayed for God to come into her life and for her to know his abundant love. When I turned to look at her, tears where flowing down her face and at that moment I saw Christ in her eyes. We prayed from that day on every time we met. It was one of the most powerful experiences I have ever felt and one I recounted two years later at her funeral when she died.

I knew there was something else out there for me to do, so imagine my delight when a year later I learned of a job working for the NHS helping those with health inequalities, especially obesity. I knew the job was mine and I had every confidence that God was directing my life through this so that I could help others. The interview process and the way I got the job is another story of God's miraculous power; however, suffice to say I got the job.

Extensive training in areas ranging from motivational interviewing, eating disorders, smoking cessation, food and mood courses, and natural juice therapy has enabled me to not only have a better relationship with food, but to realise what particular foods do to you in the addictive cycle.

I love my job, which every day is filled with God appointments. While others see fat, I see pain. While others feel ill and have pain, I see areas in which God can heal, not only emotionally but by using his food as medicine.

Daily I can come home and recount stories such as the lady who was so obese she couldn't even leave her bed, who cried with relief when I told her that I understood how she must feel. I encouraged her that I understood that it wasn't greed that got her to this place, but pain.

I met a young mother of four who already had a long history of abuse and drink and drug addiction at the age of twenty-two. I was able to tell her that she isn't a bad person for taking solace in eating when the kids have gone to bed. I could assure her that she is not alone and that there are many others who not only do the same, but that they also have immense pain in their lives.

Recently I went to see a client who proceeded to tell me her spiritual leanings as I walked in. They were very much leaning towards the occult, at which point I told her mine. "You know it's funny, I was thinking about trying out a church," she said.

I now also work with clients from the Probation Service, not for weight issues necessarily, but for their general well-being. It sometimes involves just listening to them, asking simple questions and at the end of our time together I get the opportunity to ask for feedback. I sometimes ask if I have said anything at all that may have upset or offended them.

Recently, one offender told me how much he had been helped by the conversations, as he felt that "no-one else since the age of five had treated him like a human being with feelings".

Every day I have such encounters. Every day I see God using me in small ways talking to others. Every day I see how my bad things, my secrets and my pain is helping others.

Now my dream is to work on an even larger scale helping groups of people to not only stop hating themselves, both internally and externally, but also to know there is a way to stop the cycle. Until that time, it's just one person at a time and that is powerful enough in and of itself, as God tells me regularly.

CHAPTER 4:

BIG PICTURE

Right at the beginning we observed that the Isaiah passage reflects the very core, essence and substance of who Jesus is and what he's about. This becomes our GPS, giving us a location point for all areas of life and conduct both as individuals and churches.

We have seen that the Holy Spirit is God at work, our energy source. He or she is the power behind every authentic expression of God's kingdom in the earth. The Holy Spirit works both 'on piste', through the lives of God's followers, and 'off piste', through sovereign intervention using any individual, group, event or sequence of events.

This may be at a personal or a corporate level. Wherever the goodness and the justice of God breaks out we can be sure the Holy Spirit is in the mix.

God is good and his good news encapsulates more than what we say or how we worship. It covers more than just our words, it includes our lives and lifestyles. It incorporates the way we use our homes, the way we eat, drink, fast, serve, pray, make love, do marriage, care for our children, conduct business and the way we relate to our neighbours. This good news should encapsulate all our values and the way we express them.

Supremely, this message is people-shaped. It's not made up of concepts for the 'ivory tower'. It's not merely a system of beliefs; it's far more than that. When the Christian faith is reduced in this way we often find it tempts us to tick all of its boxes, feel a little self-righteous and then use it to dismiss others who think differently.

By contrast, our faith is fuelled and energised by paradox, complexity and the all-embracing heart of God revealed in Christ. It specialises in being outside the box. This faith affirms both life and humanity because, right at the heart of his being, God has every individual in mind.

We now move on to the big picture, the grand vista. This wonderful message of Jesus doesn't just stop with the individual, but extends towards the transformation of our communities and the transformation of society.

In my spare time I run a fish farming business. It's called Future Fisheries and is dedicated to growing top-quality carp in a sustainable and responsible manner for the UK restocking market. In reality, I don't just like catching them on rod and line but I also enjoy growing fish, netting them and selling them.

A couple of years ago we were harvesting one of our sites in East Sussex. There's a two-acre lake there and I had about one hundred and eighty fish swimming around that had all been bought by one particular person. They were destined for a beautiful lake near Glastonbury in Somerset. The biggest was a forty-one-and-a-half pounder, which I was particularly proud of. I'd had it for thirteen years, from when it had weighed only a few ounces, and I was particularly pleased with myself because I was about to sell it for around £5,000! The sale price helped me face the loss of the beautiful creature I had lovingly grown and nurtured.

So, there we were, getting ready to net the lake, aided by a six-inch pump which, under normal circumstances, would have emptied the water in less than a day. This would have left us with a small puddle to net and the removal of the fish should have been easy, according to the plan! It all seemed very simple and it was of course… that is until the rain started.

This particular lake happens to be in a valley. It is fed by all the rain in the region, many surrounding springs and one particular stream. It's a stream that quickly becomes a torrent when the rain is persistent and torrential. On this particular day we started the pump and all looked good. The water immediately started to recede, so we began to prepare our nets and tanks ready to transport the fish to their new home. Then the rain started and the fun commenced!

Despite the fact that the pump was going full blast, the water level first began to even out and then, to our shock, actually began to rise – despite the fact that the pump was removing 100 litres per second, 600 litres per minute or 36,000 litres per hour. In short, it was really raining!

Meanwhile, we had our customer ready to travel to supervise the netting. He was very excited about collecting the fish but at this stage in the proceedings I began to think about how we could let him down gently. We were heading towards a flood rather than the required stable conditions for our fish harvest.

At this point my business partner Steve reluctantly intervened. "There's only one way round this, and it's through engineering. We'll cut a large hole in the dam of the lake, allow the water to drain out safely, and eventually build a 'monk,'" he said.

He went on to explain that the mediaeval monks had fish farming perfectly sussed and that originally the fish they ate on Friday were carp. They designed inline ponds with a stream coming in one end and out the other. These were created by the building of a dam, usually across a small valley. In the middle of this dam was a section where the earth was removed and a chamber was constructed from the floor of the lake to the top of the dam.

Lakeside, this consisted of one oak board on top of another. Whenever they wanted to drain the lake, they simply removed the boards, one at a time. As they did this the water level was reduced to exactly the required level, with the surplus water running through the channel in the dam into the outlet stream and away. When the fish had been removed they simply replaced the boards, the water returned to its original level and the flow of the stream coming into the lake was contained once again. The lake could then be restocked as required and the process would begin all over again.

With this system, all the monks needed to do was go up on Thursday, whip a couple of boards out of the dam, pop off to early morning prayers and by the end of prayers the water would be down, the fish could be removed and the community duly fed.

So that's what we did, but rather than constructing it by hand we hired a digger. The digger breached the dam and all the water came through. The fish followed the water congregating in a deep pool at one end of the lake, where they were duly removed and handed to a happy customer. Job done!

Since this time we have built monk systems on other lakes. One site covers more than three acres and would be unmanageable without it. We can remove the boards in the monk system at nine in the morning and by four in the afternoon the water has gone and all the fish are drained into our waiting nets by the water outlet, ready to sort and transport.

The basic moral of this story is that ancient wisdom proved that if we wanted to catch the fish we had to change the structure of the reservoir, which involved major structural change to the flow of water through the whole valley. We had to change the big structures, otherwise we would have had no chance of catching the fish.

Structural change

I believe that in the Isaiah passage we see there are some issues that have to be dealt with at the mega, structural level. If we're going to create the environment in which the good news of the kingdom can be shared, where people can be reached, then we are going to have to get involved. This involvement is not just at the micro level, but also at the macro level. Some aspects of the freedom and liberation of Jesus' manifesto cannot be fulfilled without structural change in society. In some cases this may mean legal intervention, the prosecution and exposure of perpetrators, or political action.

We're going to have to get our hands dirty and look at ways of bringing about transformation because there are many chains that manifest at a personal level in people's lives that cannot be broken without major political and social change. Where people are dominated by abusive systems, injustice, corruption, structural sin and economic oppression, the Holy Spirit is looking for those who will go, in partnership with others, to see change at the macro level.

This requires a vision that sees beyond our own personal lives and the life of our community, a vision that has a passion for society and for justice. A passion that takes us out of the black and white areas of disembodied theological or moral certainty into the grey areas of politics, complex social and moral issues and legislation. This might involve a passion for the health service, for the medical realm or for the academic realm. It's the call to get involved, get our hands dirty and make a difference. The Church is intended, as we'll see later, to be the engine room for that movement of God towards transformation in society.

The passages teach us that there's no conflict between evangelism and social action. Personal conversions and societal transformation, word and action, word and Spirit, truth and love, power evangelism and justice belong together and are built upon one another. There is no dichotomy, there's no opposition. In fact they are like water, earth and seed working together under the light of the sun to produce the crop which is God's kingdom activity in the earth.

These dimensions run seamlessly through this prophetic passage and through the ministry of Jesus. They are like different sides of the same coin, or different leaves on the same plant. Sometimes when I look at the downsides of Christian culture I wonder whether I can truly be an Evangelical or Charismatic. I am bemused by the otherworldliness of some of what is allegedly Charismatic and repulsed by the harshness and legalism of some who are allegedly Evangelical.

I believe it's hard to be an Evangelical (faithful to Scripture) without being a Charismatic (filled by, and active in, the Spirit of God), and it's hard to be a Charismatic without being an Evangelical. This is because the Holy Spirit leads you to Scripture and the Scripture leads you to the Spirit, and before you know it both Word and Spirit are woven inseparably together creating an authentic expression of spirituality. When both of these flow together, things begin to get more interesting. The Word and the Spirit do not need to be in tension, locked in some kind of status quo, as has often been portrayed by contemporary paradigms; rather they should be entwined together in an intimate relationship, coworking in the process of seeing God's will done "on earth as it is in heaven".

At our best, we stand alongside the Booths, Whitfield, Wesley and Shaftesbury. Evangelicalism is about good news for the people. The move of God's Spirit brings about liberation, justice and freedom. It's about seeing transformation. These people represent some of the best of our history and inheritance.

At our worst, it seems that we're often either caught up with merely enjoying an experience, being right, finding out who's wrong or having 'religious fisticuffs' over some irrelevant theological scenario. We fall foul of the tyranny of the either/or. There's too much dualism and not enough paradox.

God's smoothie

In this teaching, Jesus dispenses with such dualisms and creates a kind of smoothie. Now, I'm not a great smoothie fan, although my wife and daughter adore them. They love the mixture of exotic fruit whereas I prefer either a strong coffee or a beer. But what's distinctive about a smoothie is that it's a blend, and that's what we see here. Every aspect of God's kingdom is mixed together in a beautiful smoothie that's full of truth, life and power.

It energises us and sets us free personally. It sends us out into society. It causes us to think and to campaign. It drives us to intercession. It enables us to see God's power, reign and rule break out through both physical and emotional healing. But it's also about societal transformation including politics. It's about the big and the small, a wonderfully tasty smoothie!

However, sometimes we get caught in what is often called the paralysis of analysis. We dissect the beast to understand what makes its heart tick and kill it in the process.

I hear the debates: "Now, what is more important, Word or Spirit? Is it power or justice, personal salvation or caring for the poor?"

We carve up Scripture and ask which has primacy, and if we are not careful we lose the vital balance and energy of what's being presented. Here, Jesus just throws the lot into the mix, blends it together and asks us to serve it up. So let's get on with it, shall we? Let's feel free to start somewhere and in the process let's drink the whole smoothie!

Some of the dreams and the prophetic insights we've seen in Isaiah are long-term passions, including a just society. They are not things that can be achieved in a moment or indeed outside of massive social change.

Isaiah 58:6-7 reads:

Is not this the kind of fasting I have chosen:
to loose the chains of injustice
and untie the cords of the yoke,
to set the oppressed free
and to break every yoke?
Is it not to share your food with the hungry
and to provide the poor wanderer with shelter...

This teaching has to be viewed through the lens of the individual, and also through the lens of the whole people of God and society. It's not that we will Christianise society. God's kingdom is breaking in now, yet only in part. We are living in the presence of the future. We are tasting something of God's kingdom, which is yet to come in fullness. In anticipation of this fullness we are stepping out and we're living for freedom and justice in this world.

There will come a day when the kingdoms of this world will become the kingdom of our Lord and of his Christ. In the meantime we are called to live in the tension. On the one hand we are in a hurry, living urgently as if Jesus could return any second. Yet at the same time we plan for the long haul. We are like the people of God in exile, as Jeremiah describes below.

Jeremiah 29:1-7

This is the text of the letter that the prophet Jeremiah sent from Jerusalem to the surviving elders among the exiles and to the priests, the prophets and all the other people Nebuchadnezzar had carried into exile from Jerusalem to Babylon. (This was after King Jehoiachin and the queen mother, the court officials and the leaders of Judah and Jerusalem, the skilled workers and the artisans had gone into exile from Jerusalem.) He entrusted the letter to Elasah son of Shaphan and to Gemariah son of Hilkiah, whom Zedekiah king of Judah sent to King Nebuchadnezzar in Babylon. It said:

This is what the Lord Almighty, the God of Israel, says to all those I carried into exile from Jerusalem to Babylon: "Build houses and settle down; plant gardens and eat what they produce. Marry and have sons and daughters; find wives for your sons and give your daughters in marriage, so that they too may have sons and daughters. Increase in number there; do not decrease. Also, seek the peace and prosperity of the city to which I have carried you into exile. Pray to the Lord for it, because if it prospers, you too will prosper."

We're building into society, we're building into the earth because actually we are looking forward to a new heaven and a new earth. We're anticipating a physical resurrection body and a physical new heaven and a new earth. Therefore, we live in anticipation of the future and live lives committed to the freedom that will be embodied in that place. We have no idea how long it will be before this arrives, so we are digging in and building with the future in mind. We are living as if we are creating an inheritance that our sons and daughters will need to build on.

A while ago my wife and I had a romantic break in Barcelona, Spain. We had a wonderful time in that beautiful city, eating out, enjoying the culture and being together. As we toured the city we were both very inspired by the Church of the Holy Family, which was the vision of Antoni Gaudi. He set about this project fuelled by an amazing vision of what it would look like.

He had inadequate funds and resources yet persisted, and the building was never completed in his lifetime. In fact it is still incomplete. Yet the beauty and uniqueness of his vision with all its pillars and structures imitating natural forms can still be seen, and it stands as an example of his genius to this day. He had the tenacity and boldness to embark on a big vision in a similar way to our forefathers who battled against slavery as it existed in their day. He was unable to finish it but it didn't stop him trying.

Bringing transformation to individuals and communities, renewing churches, planting churches and creating spaces for God's goodness to break in takes time. Wrestling with moribund and corrupted institutions, creating life-affirming workplaces and seeking to live with integrity can be both difficult and painful.

Getting alongside the poor can be hard work. Making a difference, even with miraculous intervention, sometimes takes decades of hard work, strategy and activity. In this process, the Holy Spirit continues to come into our lives to refresh and resource us and, despite our longing for more, we find peace and contentment in just being in God and living with him.

What's your plan? I wonder if you have thought ten years into the future. If you're going to be a politician, a headmaster, help pioneer an NGO, start a local community project, foster children, be a lawyer, start a family, lead a church, be an artist or have a fish farm, you need a plan! This is because you're beginning to think big picture. You're thinking future, and no harvest comes at the click of our fingers. It takes time and investment.

I believe we need to start thinking and planning in this kind of way as we look at our nation, our communities, our families and indeed our own lives. This is because we're looking to see transformation.

Exodus people

Previously we looked at the Exodus 12, and there's something in the roots of this passage about God breaking in and effecting history. The exodus was an event that changed the future of at least two nations. We are intended to be an exodus people with an exodus message. Ultimately, we will see the nations change.

Sociologists have often analysed Christian revivals where many people have had a personal conversion experience. As they examined the data they have identified a social phenomenon called "redemption lift". Basically, what they observed was that where thousands of people genuinely experience salvation and relationship with Jesus Christ, lives are dramatically changed. People stop drinking alcohol to excess, they begin to step aside from gambling and violence, they become better husbands, wives and parents, they become more productive workers and they pay their debts. With this the whole of the society begins to change. You see a societal transformation.

Then people start to look at the macro level. They begin to enter places of influence, they begin to govern diligently and society becomes more humane and godly as a result. I don't want to be misunderstood. I don't believe we're ever going to legislate the kingdom of God. As Luther said: *"Better to have a clever Turk in power than a dumb Christian."* As Christians we have not always handled power well. However, many of our forbears have changed society with an influence that is, in essence, entirely motivated and driven by their own personal experiences of salvation at an individual level.

Sometimes we cannot free the individual without changing the society and therefore God calls us to a long-term commitment.

When Romania was first opening out to the wider world after the fall of President Ceaucescu, Rachel Bentley's Children on the Edge charity began a project there. Initially they started visiting orphanages to see what was going on. Maggie went with her on at least one occasion.

In one particular region it was discovered that there was actually systematic violence directed at the children. The key perpetrator was a man who was in authority over the orphanages.

In the words of Rachel:

> *We basically challenged his behaviour and reported him to the local (provincial) authorities. Eventually he was removed, which of course the kids just loved - they thought it was cool that Alison and I had brought this about!*

The work in Romania grew and its influence became more widespread. Rachel continues:

> *When we arrived in 1990, 'orphaned' children would be moved from institution to institution. Friends were lost and lives were thrown into upheaval as young children moved into larger*

institutions populated by older children and young adults. Working with regional and then national government we launched a pilot project to ensure these children lived in small groups with house parents (wardens).

We lobbied government to push through national legislation so that these orphans would instead be sent to a community and not orphanage school. We fought for their right to stay together as a group in one home. These struggles marked the beginning of significant change within Romania's childcare system. It culminated in the closure of many institutions, the development of family-like group homes and the growth of a new foster care system.

We brought change by identifying and working alongside significant Romanians of influence within the childcare system. This culminated in us getting to know the head of children's services for the whole country well. When Romania was drawing up its new child protection law we were given the draft by this lady for input and Stuart Gallimore, one of my friends from Revelation Church, spent one of his Christmas holidays reading it and making suggestions for improvement of the law.

This is wonderful, amazing good news! That is the gospel of the kingdom. Sometimes we have to change things at the macro level in order to see the good news experienced at grassroots.

This passage talks about "loosing the chains of injustice."

In the words of Alec Motyer: "*The abolition of what's wrong from God's perspective in social structures. Eradicating the wrong in society which crushes the liberty of others.*"

Genuine moves of the Holy Spirit will always have this right at their heart.

Abolitionism is our inheritance. We should look at Wilberforce, whose life is portrayed in the film *Amazing Grace*. Today, God is calling us as a Church to a new abolitionism because as someone (believed by many to be Edmund Burke) once said:

"All that is required for evil to prosper is for good men to do nothing."

Some friends of mine made a film called *Call and Response*, dedicated to the eradication of twenty-first-century slavery and the powerful declaration of the movie is:

"Justice is what love looks like in public."

If we want to take the love of God into the public domain, justice is a key place to start.

I believe that this is a message that will resonate in the hearts of many within the younger generation. I have been involved a lot in university work over the last ten or twelve years and there's a hunger for God, which is often seen in the form of a hunger for justice. There isn't the same urgency or feeling among people to engage with some of the older apologetic questions, such as: *"What about the Bible and science?"* or *"Did the resurrection literally and physically happen?"*

Often the response to these debates is: "So what!" These issues still require our attention but answering them will no longer scratch people's itch. However, right at the heart of humanity is a craving for justice.

I believe that, as we go forward with the message of Jesus, this is something that will resonate very deeply in the hearts of this generation.

Launching pads

However, we need strong and resourceful churches that are able to use their resources and mobilise their communities for this cause. There's no sacred and secular divide through the middle of culture. The calling of the Church to worship and for mission includes every aspect of this manifesto.

There's a direct link between God's prophetic Spirit speaking into the lives of individuals and bringing about transformation more broadly. There needs to be a flexibility in vision and vocation as people move between their church communities and society at large.

This doesn't mean that you have to have a secular vocation or that the most important vocation is that of minister, pastor or church leader. Whichever you are called to at this moment is the most important one for you. If you feel flexible, you can do both! You can lead a church, plant a church and start a business. You can be a mayor, a school governor, a politician and you can lead a community. All of these are consistent with God's heart for people and, in my experience, can flow well together if we live in the light of this paradigm.

We also need to beware of the swinging pendulum. Some complain: *"The Church is irrelevant - we must engage with society."*

A reaction then follows, during which people feel they need to disengage from church only to find that without spiritual community they are alone, less effective, vulnerable and drying up.

Others get so absorbed in 'churchy business' that they forget about what we are here for. A closed, often self-perpetuating system develops, which in the end becomes stagnant and ineffective.

The reservoir of the Holy Spirit is located within this tension. The kingdom community requires investment, strength and commitment; not as an end in itself but so it can fulfil its destiny as a force for personal and social transformation (salvation).

So as a normal part of the life of our church gatherings, whether big or small, congregational or small-group-based we need to be asking:

"What's going on in your life and business? How can we pray for you, support and anoint you to be effective for God in all these areas? Who among your friends and contacts should we be praying over for God's blessing and that they may get to know God for themselves?"

How can we resource each other in the workplace, in business and in different areas of influence? How can we support one another as we touch the lives of ordinary people, day in day out? How can our prayers, prophesies and resources create communities of 'sent ones', going out in the name of Jesus Christ to make a difference?

How can we keep reporting back and hearing people's stories, which in turn energise us to keep moving? How can we create environments where the deep questions and struggles people face, as they engage with the pain, paradox and grey areas of our world, can surface and be processed without resorting to cheap fixes and trite answers?

It's not good to have churchless philanthropists, and there are a few of them out there who just don't feel like they fit into church because they sit in church meetings thinking:

"How does what I'm passionate about and called to relate to this religious club?"

We've got to bridge the gap, because actually there's something in our DNA and identity as kingdom churches that means we are here to make a difference. We can be an engine room for the activity of God in the earth. The kingdom of God is God's reign and rule in the earth, mediated by the Holy Spirit. He creates and catalyses the Church and change in society.

Jesus' miracles are examples of what society is like when God is fully King. The blind see, the hungry are fed, the lame walk. As churches we seek the kingdom, we proclaim the kingdom, we're an agent of the kingdom but we're not the kingdom itself. We have the call to outwork a kingdom-oriented vocation by creating communities that incarnate and proclaim the manifesto of the King.

At the same time we create environments in businesses, charities, teams and relationships where God's reign and rule can come. We're creating the right conditions through prayer, spiritual warfare, going out on the streets, laying hands on people and seeing people saved. We are engaging in just trade, making good investments, creating fulfilling work opportunities, facing complex issues, developing relevant apologetics and lining up Scripture with what's going on in society.

We begin to push outwards and, as we do so, we create the conditions that enable the Holy Spirit to come in greater power. That's what we should be about as it is what we're here for.

Freedom

We're called to *"untie the cords of a yoke"* (Isaiah 58:6). The yoke was used to tie up an animal. This means to literally *eliminate every way in which people are treated like animals.*

We must live with the belief that every human being, no matter how broken, has been created in the image of God. We're here to loose the chains and to cry freedom! The word freedom in the Greek manuscript is "manumission" – "freedom". There's a nightclub in Ibiza called Manumission. Its branding is all about sexual bondage and immorality. We're called to propagate a different type of freedom; a freedom that rejects the objectifying of individuals sexually, which leads to all sorts of personal and social dysfunction.

We need to realise that the good news stands for itself. We are here to release the captives and prisoners. Isaiah 42:6-7 reads:

> *"I, the Lord, have called you in righteousness;*
> *I will take hold of your hand.*
> *I will keep you and will make you to be a covenant for the people*
> *and a light for the Gentiles,*
> *to open eyes that are blind,*
> *to free captives from prison*
> *and to release from the dungeon those who sit in darkness."*

This captivity and these prisons mean literally *'a bondage imposed by people and place'*. It's relational bondage. Bondage within every sphere be it family life, within the workplace or from the government. Indeed, it includes all that might oppress. It can be a societal bondage whether it is based on economics or around race or gender. This gospel of God's love breaks open the prisons and releases captives.

When reading *The Times* online one day I came across an article by politician and writer Matthew Parris, which is quite remarkable. It would be fair to say that he's not coming from the position where he's professing faith, or would indeed endorse a great deal of what I've written here. However, I think this article expresses much of what I've been illustrating in this chapter, so I've included some excerpts here.

The article, written after a trip to Malawi, reveals some interesting insights:

> *It inspired me, renewing my flagging faith in development charities. But travelling in Malawi refreshed another belief, too: one I've been trying to banish all my life, but an observation I've been unable to avoid since my African childhood. It confounds my ideological beliefs, stubbornly refuses to fit my world view, and has embarrassed my growing belief that there is no God.*
>
> *Now a confirmed atheist, I've become convinced of the enormous contribution that Christian evangelism makes in Africa: sharply distinct from the work of secular NGOs, government projects and international aid efforts. These alone will not do. Education and training alone will not do. In Africa, Christianity changes people's hearts. It brings a spiritual transformation. The rebirth is real. The change is good.*

He adds:

> *First, then, the observation. We had friends who were missionaries, and as a child I stayed often with them; I also stayed, alone with my little brother, in a traditional rural African village. In the city we had working for us Africans who had converted and were strong believers. The Christians were always different. Far from having cowed or confined its converts, their faith appeared to have liberated and relaxed them. There was a liveliness, a curiosity, an engagement with the world, a directness in their dealings with others that seemed to be missing in traditional African life. They stood tall.*

According to Parris:

> *Whenever we entered a territory worked by missionaries, we had to acknowledge that something changed in the faces of the people we passed and spoke to: something in their eyes, the way they approached you direct, man-to-man, without looking down or away. They had not become more deferential towards strangers - in some ways less so - but more open.*
>
> *It would suit me to believe that their honesty, diligence and optimism in their work was unconnected with personal faith. Their work was secular, but surely affected by what they were. What they were was, in turn, influenced by a conception of man's place in the Universe that Christianity had taught.*
>
> *Anxiety - fear of evil spirits, of ancestors, of nature and the wild, of a tribal hierarchy, of quite everyday things - strikes deep into the whole structure of rural African thought. Every man has his place and, call it fear or respect, a great weight grinds down the individual spirit, stunting curiosity. People*

> *won't take the initiative, won't take things into their own hands or on their own shoulders.*

Parris concludes:

> *Christianity, post-Reformation and post-Luther, with its teaching of a direct, personal, two-way link between the individual and God, unmediated by the collective, and insubordinate to any other human being, smashes straight through the philosophical/spiritual framework I've just described. It offers something to hold on to to those anxious to cast off a crushing tribal groupthink. That is why and how it liberates.*
>
> *Those who want Africa to walk tall amid twenty-first-century global competition must not kid themselves that providing the material means or even the knowhow that accompanies what we call development will make the change. A whole belief system must first be supplanted.*
>
> *And I'm afraid it has to be supplanted by another. Removing Christian evangelism from the African equation may leave the continent at the mercy of a malign fusion of Nike, the witch doctor, the mobile phone and the machete.*

This is a wonderful encouragement for us! We can have confidence in the gospel. Confidence in this good news we have been given. It is not just powerful in changing individuals' lives, but as we grapple with this as the Church and proclaim it widely we will indeed see transformation in our society.

However, we have some choices to make. We need to take some steps to participate in and identify with the world around us, following the example of Jesus who was "made flesh" (John 1:14).

Sometimes we live under the myth that somehow we can be truly objective. That somehow we can withdraw from the world and take off the lenses of our culture and upbringing, observing the world with pure rationality, and therefore understanding everything that's going on.

Of course, the difficulty that we all have as human beings is that we are all part of the world, we are products of our culture and our lenses are coloured by our lives and experiences. We cannot separate ourselves. We are influenced by our upbringing, by our moods and by our emotions, and this is reflected in all our positions, morally, theologically and relationally. Yet we live under this myth of objectivity. If we continue to live this way, without humility, it creates some very unhealthy traits in our lives and in our spirituality.

We attempt to analyse the world around us and, as something or someone attracts our attention, sadly we can retreat into a 'certainty' that's more to do with our own preconceived ideas than it is to do with God's truth. This can apply to our attitudes to the poor, those who are different from us and those who see the world or indeed any situation differently. We then endeavour perhaps to defend the 'rightness' of our certainty or make any dissenting voices or loose ends 'wrong' according to our 'objective' assessment.

If we see something as wrong, our reactions are often defensive and fearful. We look at people in our communities who live differently and we perhaps disagree with their lifestyle choices, morality or culture. We then often project our own fear onto them and we make them the enemy, putting barriers up in our hearts and lives.

Then, finally, what happens? We withdraw. We end up with a Christianity that's fearful and withdrawn, separated from mainstream culture. We become ineffective and unable to be agents for change. We cannot learn to explore the command of Jesus to "love our enemies" (Matthew 5:43) from this position.

What is a better way? What is the Jesus-centred way to operate? Jesus shows us the way of love and acceptance. He accepts us and, as we receive his acceptance, we are increasingly able to accept others just as they are. We love them, we get alongside them.

Then what happens if you accept someone? You begin to identify with them. In the incarnation, Jesus identified with humanity and suffered with us. As we enter people's worlds rather than judging them from a withdrawn position of fear, we begin to suffer by experiencing all their dilemmas and contradictions. We suffer a little with them but are enabled to communicate God's manifesto from the position of relational connection and understanding.

Our worldview comes in alongside the worldview of others and our beliefs, experiences and faith are stretched and sometimes shaken. As we begin to experience truth in the way it's meant to be experienced, in life, we get alongside people and we suffer with them as we enter their worlds.

This is what God did for us. God did not sit there in heaven, separate and apart from humanity in rational perfection. He entered our world and he accepted us. He identified with us and he suffered with us saying, "Come, follow me".

Jim McNeish would say that this is the healthy way to lead. That if you want to influence, manage staff or build teams, you have to be incarnational. If we live defensively, afraid of pain, we are in many ways losing out on what it means to be alive. God entered the world through Christ in the incarnation, identified with us and showed us what it means to be alive. The experience of pain is part of being alive.

So if we're going to see society transformed, we're going to have to enter the world and engage with people's lives. This is not as difficult as it seems; believe it or not, we are all in the world already, even if some Christians behave otherwise!

To bring good news we've got to enter people's lives. We have to enter the philosophical realm, the psychosexual clinic and many other places. We have to get alongside the person that's dying. We have to enter people's worlds, meet them as human beings and connect with them. We need to engage with the big issues without fear but conscious of the pain. In doing so we follow in the footsteps of Jesus.

In the words of Helen Keller:

"Security is mostly a superstition. It does not exist in nature, nor do the children of men as a whole experience it. Avoiding danger is no safer in the long run than outright exposure. Life is either a daring adventure, or nothing."

POSTCARDS FROM MY FRIENDS · RACHEL BENTLEY

We have known Rachel Bentley for more than twenty years and have walked the journey of church together for that entire period. In fact, we are still in the same cell group. Here are some of her experiences at Children on the Edge.

In my twenty years of working for the rights of marginalised children – literally those 'on the edge' of life, in every corner of the globe – I have seen unjust laws repealed and new laws brought in: laws that have gone on to improve those children's lives, freeing and releasing their futures. But such changes rarely start at the top, they begin at the grassroots.

The changes in Romanian law mentioned earlier in this chapter came about after an encounter with children living in one orphanage, in one rural village in Romania.

Understanding, then trying to help their plight, led us to focus on changing a national law – a change which later affected the lives of thousands of children without parental care.

But to effect that change and make a real difference, we had to work from the ground up. Change at local level and then provincial level. The structural change at that level then influenced Romania's new child protection laws.

As an organisation we did not set out to change that national law. Instead, we focused on the grassroots issues, getting our hands dirty and working faithfully, day in and day out, facing many obstacles and challenges. Along the way a model of good practice was developed for these forty-four children, which brought about that provincial and then national change.

We were not focusing on changing a nation but were faced with the real needs of a few children: those in front of us. To bring real change to their lives necessitated changing laws and practice in Romanian childcare.

Developing this model of good practice attracted the attention of key people in positions of power. Admittedly, initially, they were few and far between. But slowly we found them or they found us. Together, over the course of many years, we worked together to bring about significant change.

One of the most striking examples of this effort is the story of Lucia Gavrilita. Lucia is a Christian lady living in Moldova. She gave birth to two children with special needs. It was through her determination to help them that she realised that many other Moldovan children needed such help. Not only this, she understood that the key to such change, and bringing about any hope for children such as her own, required the law to be changed too.

At Children on the Edge we have helped fund some of the work of her charity, Speranta, which means "hope" in Romanian. Later, she would go on to become a government minister, a testament to her will and determination. However, Lucia told us that the most vital support she has had has been our friendship; standing alongside her in her battles, being there as a sounding board, offering wisdom when we had it. I will never forget the time a colleague and I sat and talked and prayed with her for an hour in her plush ministerial office while her door was shut because it was a "very important meeting"!

I will let journalist Cahal Milmo take up her story as told in the Independent on December 21, 2010:

On a spring day in 1994, doctors sat Lucia Gavrilita down and told her that her life was being ruined by her disabled son and daughter. Rather than waste their time with attempts to improve her children's condition, they stated bluntly she should take up an offer to send them away to a state-run home.

It would have been easy for the languages teacher, at the time aged twenty-two, to accept the brutally perfunctory advice of the medical professionals in her native Moldova. For decades the policy in this former Soviet satellite state, now one of Europe's poorest countries, had been to consign its disabled children to large under-funded and ill-equipped boarding homes where "care" consisted of sufficient food and medication to keep inhabitants docile.

Thousands of parents before Lucia had surrendered their offspring rather than face the life poverty and the absence of support that would follow if they chose to keep them at home. Those born different, she was told, have no place in normal family life.

But Lucia refused.

With this refusal – made despite the devastating effects of the rare genetic disorder that had struck her then three-year-old son, Calin, and one-year-old daughter, Elena – began a tumultuous and extraordinary struggle that brought this iron-willed housewife to the brink of suicide.

Remarkably, it has also transported her from the Stalinist tenement block on the edge of the Moldovan capital, Chisinau, where she lives with her family to the neo-classical splendour of the office of the country's prime minister and her very own government ministry.

Some sixteen years after the doctors first effectively told Lucia to dispose of her son and daughter, she has produced a remarkable transformation, not only in the destiny and treatment of her own children but for every one of the fifteen thousand special needs children in Moldova, by changing the nation's attitude to disability.

As well as providing the blueprint for a nationwide network of day centres run by parents and volunteers, she has used her surprise political appointment as Moldova's deputy disability minister to produce the country's first law laying down basic rights and standards for those with disabilities.

It is a battle to crush taboos and prejudices that she looks back on with a degree of disbelief as she sits in the headquarters of her charity, Speranta, housed in what was once her family apartment.

Speaking with the sort of unwavering candour that has become her trademark, she said: "After my children were born, we had a visit every three months to the hospital for treatment. But when my son was three, after one of these sessions I went to make my next appointment and was told that it was not a reasonable thing to do.

"The doctors said they could see no improvement and that it was waste of my time and theirs to continue. They said that I and my husband were still young and if we kept these two children it would destroy our life. They offered us places in an institution.

"At first, I thought maybe I should take their advice but then I looked at the homes and saw that Calin and Elena would not even be together because the institutions were for boys and girls. It was a terrible realisation – from that moment forth I decided I would fight for my children. I just didn't realise how hard I would have to fight."

From the start, the odds have been against Lucia.

Calin, now nineteen, and Elena, seventeen, were born with a congenital disorder of glycosylation, which affects the body's ability to process proteins at a cellular level, resulting in multiple disorders ranging from a lack of basic reflexes, such as the ability to swallow, to a likelihood that any male sufferer will go blind by their eighteenth birthday. It is incredibly rare – there are just two hundred confirmed cases in the world.

In 1991, when Calin was born, Moldova had secured independence following the collapse of the Soviet Union, but the Communist-era attitude that disabled children should be medicated and hidden persisted long after the disappearance of the politburo and a centrally planned economy. Lucia, now thirty-eight, embarked on a crash course in modern techniques to deal with disability, attending sessions for medical students at a specialist centre in neighbouring Romania and signing up at Chisinau's medical university. When combined with the sixteen hours of daily treatment that her children required, it brought her – and her marriage – to breaking point.

Speaking in the fluent English she taught herself to understand medical text books, she said: "I was completely focused on the children. It was so demanding that we had no sort of home life. My husband wanted to leave – the marriage was too much. It was then that I decided I had to find other people with disabled children so we could help each other."

The result was what became Speranta. Lucia found a way round her hatred of cooking by making common cause with a mother who was a professional cook. Through a friend she found a mother of a disabled child who was a doctor and could perform physiotherapy.

Together, this group of volunteers ran a day centre in Lucia's sitting room for six children, begging and borrowing equipment from foreign donors including the British charity Children on the Edge, and rapidly establishing an organisation built on an unblinking policy of professionalism. Lucia persuaded organisations abroad to send her qualified physiotherapists, paediatricians, psychologists and carers as volunteers to tutor her burgeoning organisation in state-of-the art techniques.

Within three years of its foundation in 1998, Speranta had opened two more centres and diverted dozens of children away from the inadequacies of state-run homes, where residents sleep in dormitories and receive little specialised care. As Lucia puts it: "If you enter one of these institutions with a mild disability, the likelihood is you won't leave and the disability will get worse."

Fired by her success with Speranta, Lucia was determined to demolish more of the structure built up by Moldovan society to exclude those with disabilities, securing a place in a mainstream school for Calin in 2000. The scheme has since mushroomed into Moldova's first to place special needs pupils in conventional secondary schools, offering three hundred and fifty children a place in society that would hitherto have been denied them.

Lucia said: "Even today, I get people who ask me, 'Why do you try to integrate these children?' I tell them it is because they are human beings and human beings are social beings. They should be part of our society, not hidden away."

But despite the success of Speranta, fate was not finished with Lucia.

On December 3, 2007, Moldova's then Communist President, Vladimir Voronin, visited the care centre to mark International Day for Disabled Persons.

By the time he left the building, having been reduced to tears by what he said was the sight for the first time in his life of a disabled child smiling, he had offered Lucia a ministerial post in the government in charge of disabled affairs.

After debating whether to take the post, the woman who started her struggle on behalf of her children and slept on the floor of her sitting room after giving her home over to volunteers found herself negotiating the twisted corridors of political power in Moldova to change the law.

It has not been an easy process. Although senior figures such as Mr Voronin accepted her arguments that providing home-based care for the disabled would cost one-tenth of what the cash-strapped Moldovan government spent on its boarding homes, a mixture of obdurate bureaucracy and the global recession made obtaining the initial investment to reform the system an impossible task.

Recalling her arrival at the Ministry of Social Protection, Lucia said: "Suddenly, I was in this huge building where everybody wore suits. I found myself asking why God had put me in this place. I was a minister without a department. I wanted to create a department that dealt only with disability but this was during the economic crisis and everyone was being asked for cuts of twenty percent. I was told to go to the Ministry of Finance, which I knew was the same as being told to go away."

What those who sought to obstruct the new deputy minister for disability did not bargain for was the fact that the new minister of finance was one Mariana Durlesteanu, Moldova's former ambassador to London and the mother of a disabled child. Lucia and Mariana had known each other for years, not least because the ambassador had been instrumental in obtaining help for Speranta from British charities.

Within a matter of weeks, Lucia had secured the investment she needed to start her department with a dedicated staff and began to draw up the first nationwide strategy enshrining in Moldovan law the UN Convention on Disability Rights, which confers basic state-funded entitlements on those with special needs.

Lucia left her ministry last year after a change of government but not before the legislation she created was passed into law. It is a monumental achievement for a woman who while battling in high office has had to continue meeting the needs of her children. She said: "The law is an instrument for change. It is an important step towards changing attitudes but only a first step."

International experts say that Lucia's success should not be underestimated. Rachel Bentley, director of Children on the Edge, said: "She is one those rare individuals you meet in life, a mum who gave birth to two children with special needs who decided not just to help her own but all such children in her nation. A truly selfless, dedicated and inspiring woman, like social reformers of old, she has brought change to a nation and thousands of children's lives."

Beneath the apparently impregnable exterior, Lucia does not hide her vulnerabilities or the personal cost of spending nearly two decades in an uphill and at times overwhelming struggle.

Describing the point at which she realised that the baby Elena had the same disorder as her brother, Lucia said: "It was devastating. I was at the end of my tether. I cried for a week and I thought several times I would end my life. People can be cruel. I spoke to a priest and he told me that I had these children because I was paying the price for a sin, that it was a curse."

By trial and error, Lucia has learnt to deal with her children's condition, which changes as they grow older. A recent crisis with Elena's ability to absorb calcium has been improved vastly by swapping to a strict vegan diet, while Calin's sight has been improved by the unorthodox method of eating quails' eggs.

But the true nature of her achievement is more elemental. In short, it will mean that never again will a doctor stand before a parent in Moldova and advise them to surrender their child to a state that wants to hide their offspring away.

Lucia said: "I lead a very busy life. I have to write down everything on 'to-do' lists. Otherwise it is overwhelming. But everything, absolutely everything, has been for my children."

CHAPTER 5:
ECONOMY

So, we have a messenger who's the Messiah, God with us, revealed to us, and a message that's his manifesto. It's the essence and the core of what faith in God should represent. We shouldn't be distracted from this focus and as we engage with other issues we do so with the lens of Jesus Christ firmly in mind. If we want to be on-message, close to the heart of Christ and hanging out in the presence of the Holy Spirit, then this is the direction we must take.

This message is people-shaped. It's not primarily about concepts, abstract theories or dogma; this message is about people. It's about every human being that has ever lived and will ever be born, people that Jesus has died for. He opens up the way to relationship with God through faith in him, which is the door into eternity. But it doesn't stop with the individual. It's not an individualistic message. It's a message that affects our relationships, families, careers and our communities. It spills out towards the transformation of society.

The last major theme I want to consider is that this message brings with it an 'economy'. The manifesto of Jesus is about the 'economy of God'.

In the light of the instability of our current global situation there's always plenty of talk around economic matters, particularly within media and government. We have currently moved from 'quantitative easing', which is basically printing more money, into the phase of 'my cuts are better than your cuts'. This is a time of very painful global financial 'cardiac arrest'. It's the precursor to a radical lifestyle readjustment, particularly in the West, with literally whole nations being bailed out to avoid bankruptcy.

Clearly there's something badly wrong with the world's economic systems. I'm not about to offer an in-depth prognosis here as I'm no economist and wouldn't know where to start. One thing is for sure: we need economists with a vision of the future that is shaped by the heart of God and is both adapted and counter-cultural enough to plot a way forward. A system that's dominated by acquisitiveness, self-interest and the profit motive is never going to imbibe the kingdom of God. That doesn't mean, however, that we cannot see a level of righteousness and justice outworked that could change the circumstances of ordinary people at grass roots on a global scale.

Amid all this talk about the economy we should note that God has his own economy. Something he has established in creation, foreshadowed in the Old Testament and fulfilled in Christ. The core values we encounter here should shape the essence of our micro economies as Christians; be this at a personal or community (church) level. This economy has been given to us, his Church, in the good news of the gospel. We are commissioned to live it out in this world in anticipation of the time when God's kingdom comes in all its fullness.

At times, God's economy appears upside-down and illogical

when compared with how our world operates. Certainly it's very different, but bearing in mind the dysfunction of the current global systems, maybe it's worth a look?

I love the book of Philippians. Only in God's economy can a book on freedom be written from a prison cell. That's the quality of God's economy. Because even if the worst-case scenario occurs, humanly speaking, nothing can rob us of the freedom and power that Christ has given us through the Holy Spirit. Even in prison we can be free as a bird. The apostle Paul says:

"I have learned the secret of being content in all situations" (Philippians 4:12-13).

The year of the Lord's favour

As we anchor ourselves again in Luke 4:19 and Isaiah 61:2 we see Jesus proclaiming the "year of the Lord's favour". In the words of venture capitalist and Christian author Kim Tan:

"It is clear that by the time of Jesus people understood Isaiah 58:6 and 61:1-2 as reinterpreting Leviticus 25 so that the age of salvation would be the age of final Jubilee, of God's breaking in reign."

Most commentators would see that Jesus is referring to the year of Jubilee. A year that, although God instituted it in the Old Testament, was never implemented by Israel as far as we know. Jesus then basically comes out and says:

"Look, this year of Jubilee is fulfilled in me."

We don't have space here to explore in depth how the old covenant, the law and the new covenant dovetail together and how they are fulfilled in Christ. What I want to do here is to explain a little about the Jubilee, about the Sabbaths and draw some principles that I hope will inspire us. There is room for many different ways of outworking these principles. I hope we will see some glimpses of what God's economy might mean for our lives, which is an incredibly exciting prospect. To read further on the Jubilee it's worth looking at *The Jubilee Gospel* by Kim Tan and the chapter covering it in *The Mission of God* by author and missionary theologian Christopher Wright.

The year of Jubilee fits the rhythm of Sabbath given by God to the Jewish nation in the Old Testament. There was a weekly Sabbath, an annual Sabbath every seven years, and every fifty years there was a Jubilee Sabbath. The land Sabbath law is similar to the weekly Sabbath.

Exodus 23:10-13 gives an outline:

> *"For six years you are to sow your fields and harvest the crops, but during the seventh year let the land lie unploughed and unused. Then the poor among your people may get food from it, and the wild animals may eat what is left. Do the same with your vineyard and your olive grove.*
>
> *"Six days do your work, but on the seventh day do not work, so that your ox and your donkey may rest, and so that the slave born in your household and the foreigner living among you may be refreshed.*
>
> *"Be careful to do everything I have said to you."*

Here we see a rhythm that God is bringing into the life and culture of Israel. It brings with it a sense of sustainability, both in terms of human relationships and the wider creation. It makes a lot of sense. Anybody who works in farming would be familiar with crop rotation and the benefits of leaving fields fallow after a period of sustained production.

The same principle works well in fish farming, where ponds are often left dry after a season of production to allow grasses to grow which, as the lake is refilled, rot down and create a flourish of nutrients, ensuring a lush environment within which microorganisms proliferate. This creates plenty of food for the next batch of fish and every other creature that is sustained by the aquatic environment.

Basically, the Sabbath laws are about sustainability. There are rhythms that God as creator has enshrined and programmed into creation. Just as the progression of the seasons paves the way for seedtime and harvest year on year, so the Sabbath rhythms built into creation provide a framework for functionality and wellbeing. The Sabbath rhythm and rhythms of life are not just important for human beings, they are there for the benefit of the whole of creation, not only that, the whole of creation unconsciously yearns for the fullness of God's Sabbath rest, for which it was ultimately created.

How would it be if Sabbath principles were integrated into human resources policies, working and trading patterns? My belief is that God's order would enhance human wellbeing, performance, productivity and fulfilment, with the resultant benefits to the bottom line. More importantly, it would provide major benefits for the whole of humanity and society, bringing peace and wholeness (shalom) into the everyday. This is the 'feel-good factor' individuals, families and governments alike are seeking and it's found supremely in Christ.

Leviticus 25:1-7 describes the land Sabbath:

> *The Lord said to Moses at Mount Sinai, "Speak to the Israelites and say to them: 'When you enter the land I am going to give you, the land itself must observe a Sabbath to the Lord. For six years sow your fields, and for six years prune your vineyards and gather their crops. But in the seventh year the land is to have a year of Sabbath rest, a Sabbath to the Lord.*
>
> *Do not sow your fields or prune your vineyards. Do not reap what grows of itself or harvest the grapes of your untended vines. The land is to have a year of rest. Whatever the land yields during the Sabbath year will be food for you—for yourself, your male and female servants, and the hired worker and temporary resident who live among you, as well as for your livestock and the wild animals in your land. Whatever the land produces may be eaten.'"*

Jubilee is a process that's in place for the sake of all people, including the poor, the alien and the environment. It's easy to see the common sense and the beauty and the rhythm of God within this law and I think it requires some thought as to how we run with the heart of it. Who are the "workers, servants and temporary residents" among us and how do we respond to them?

God's law in its entirety is good and pure. Our problem is that we can't fulfil it in our own strength, we always mess up. The apostle Paul infers that the law is like a guardian that leads us to Christ – to the grace of Christ, the cross of Christ and the forgiveness of Christ, because the law itself is fulfilled in him. When we then hear the "new commandment" (John 13:34) Jesus gives us and we begin to experience the reign of the Holy Spirit, some of these principles come back to us through the lens of Jesus and in the light of the New Testament. These are still there for us to outwork as part of our mission.

The seventh year is called the "year for cancelling debts" in Deuteronomy 15:1-11.

> *At the end of every seven years you must cancel debts. This is how it is to be done: every creditor shall cancel any loan they have made to a fellow Israelite. They shall not require payment from anyone among their own people, because the Lord's time for cancelling debts has been proclaimed. You may require payment from a foreigner, but you must cancel any debt your fellow Israelite owes you.*
>
> *However, there need be no poor people among you, for in the land the Lord your God is giving you to possess as your inheritance, he will richly bless you, if only you fully obey the Lord your God and are careful to follow all these commands I am giving you today. For the Lord your God will bless you as he has promised, and you will lend to many nations but will borrow from none. You will rule over many nations but none will rule over you.*
>
> *If anyone is poor among your fellow Israelites in any of the towns of the land the Lord your God is giving you, do not be hardhearted or tight fisted toward them. Rather, be open-handed and freely lend them whatever they need. Be careful not to harbour this wicked thought: "The seventh year, the year for cancelling debts, is near," so that you do not show ill will toward the needy among your fellow Israelites and give them nothing. They may then appeal to the Lord against you, and you will be found guilty of sin.*

> *Give generously to them and do so without a grudging heart; then because of this the Lord your God will bless you in all your work and in everything you put your hand to. There will always be poor people in the land. Therefore I command you to be open-handed toward your fellow Israelites who are poor and needy in your land.*

In this year, all debts are redeemed. So in the seventh year, any remaining debt is cleared. Imagine what would happen within family life, relationships and community, never mind the economy, if this was implemented. The gap between the rich and poor would be sliced, so much injustice would be removed and society at large would be characterised by a greater equality and quality of life. Many political revolutions would be rendered unnecessary and so much social strife would be eradicated. You can see why the Israelites struggled to implement this one. Those who hold the power would find it very difficult to embrace something that would limit their control and the acquisition of unlimited riches.

In the New Testament, Jesus uses the word for forgive, "aphesis" (Luke 7:47), which means the release or cancellation of debts. Furthermore, he uses the parable of the two debtors in Luke 7: 41-43 to explain God's forgiveness of the 'sinful' woman against the backdrop of the Jubilee approach to debt cancellation.

> *"Two people owed money to a certain moneylender. One owed him five hundred denarii, [about a day's wages] and the other fifty. Neither of them had the money to pay him back, so he forgave the debts of both. Now which of them will love him more?"*
>
> *Simon replied, "I suppose the one who had the bigger debt forgiven."*

"You have judged correctly," Jesus said.

God's values around forgiveness seem to have the same pattern and outcome within both relational grievances and financial matters. Once more we see that the Jesus-centred view of life is more integrated, more holistic than most Christian teaching would have the ability to recognise. This is because we often come to God with unconscious, inherited preconceived ideas. These are the air that we have breathed since childhood and when we come to Scripture we view it with these lenses firmly in place. We need help!

However, underlying Jubilee is a radical shift in how we view ownership and also debt.

Last year I bought a forty-acre site with my friend and business partner, which contains a thirty-acre lake. It's a beautiful site full of a rich array of flora, fauna, insect and bird life, deer, foxes and most importantly big fish!

Although in the eyes of English law we own the site, we have often expressed together how we feel like we are merely stewards, investing and nurturing it for those that follow after, creating and safeguarding the environment for the many creatures who outwork their life rhythms in harmony with the ecology of the lake, largely unnoticed by humanity. It feels as though we are not in control, neither should we be. We are custodians, but in these terms God is the owner. This is the cosmic, economic, social and relational framework given by the Jubilee. It has the potential to revolutionise the way we look at life.

So we come to Leviticus 25:8-55, the pièce de résistance that describes the Jubilee Sabbath. God says:

"Count off seven Sabbath years—seven times seven years—so that the seven Sabbath years amount to a period of forty-nine years. Then have the trumpet sounded everywhere on the tenth day of the seventh month; on the Day of Atonement sound the trumpet throughout your land. Consecrate the fiftieth year and proclaim liberty throughout the land to all its inhabitants.

"It shall be a Jubilee for you; each of you is to return to your family property and to your own clan. The fiftieth year shall be a Jubilee for you; do not sow and do not reap what grows of itself or harvest the untended vines. For it is a Jubilee and is to be holy for you; eat only what is taken directly from the fields.

"In this year of Jubilee everyone is to return to their own property.

"If you sell land to any of your own people or buy land from them, do not take advantage of each other. You are to buy from your own people on the basis of the number of years since the Jubilee. And they are to sell to you on the basis of the number of years left for harvesting crops. When the years are many, you are to increase the price, and when the years are few, you are to decrease the price, because what is really being sold to you is the number of crops. Do not take advantage of each other, but fear your God. I am the Lord your God.

"Follow my decrees and be careful to obey my laws, and you will live safely in the land. Then the land will yield its fruit, and you will eat your fill and live there in safety. You may ask, 'What will we eat in the seventh year if we do not plant or harvest our crops?' I will send you such a blessing in the sixth year that the land will yield enough for three years. While you plant during the eighth year, you will eat from the old crop and will continue

to eat from it until the harvest of the ninth year comes in.

"The land must not be sold permanently, because the land is mine and you reside in my land as foreigners and strangers. Throughout the land that you hold as a possession, you must provide for the redemption of the land.

"If one of your fellow Israelites becomes poor and sells some of their property, their nearest relative is to come and redeem what they have sold. If, however, there is no one to redeem it for them but later on they prosper and acquire sufficient means to redeem it themselves, they are to determine the value for the years since they sold it and refund the balance to the one to whom they sold it; they can then go back to their own property. But if they do not acquire the means to repay, what was sold will remain in the possession of the buyer until the Year of Jubilee. It will be returned in the Jubilee, and they can then go back to their property.

"Anyone who sells a house in a walled city retains the right of redemption a full year after its sale. During that time the seller may redeem it. If it is not redeemed before a full year has passed, the house in the walled city shall belong permanently to the buyer and the buyer's descendants. It is not to be returned in the Jubilee. But houses in villages without walls around them are to be considered as belonging to the open country. They can be redeemed, and they are to be returned in the Jubilee.

"The Levites always have the right to redeem their houses in the Levitical towns, which they possess. So the property of the Levites is redeemable—that is, a house sold in any town they hold—and is to be returned in the Jubilee, because the houses in the towns of the Levites are their property among the Israelites. But

the pastureland belonging to their towns must not be sold; it is their permanent possession.

"If any of your fellow Israelites become poor and are unable to support themselves among you, help them as you would a foreigner and stranger, so they can continue to live among you. Do not take interest or any profit from them, but fear your God, so that they may continue to live among you. You must not lend them money at interest or sell them food at a profit. I am the Lord your God, who brought you out of Egypt to give you the land of Canaan and to be your God."

In the fiftieth year everything goes back to where it started. Everything that's been acquired by anybody over that fifty-year period returns to its original owner. Where some people have succeeded, their wealth is redistributed: others who have fallen into poverty are restored. Some people may have become incredibly rich while others are destitute. At the end of fifty years everything starts again. This process is made fair economically, encouraging entrepreneurial activity in that the value of land is dictated by the value and number of crops remaining until the Jubilee year.

Here we have a law for God's people that enshrines equality, justice and care for the poor. It also has something very interesting to say about ownership, particularly in relation to land. Imagine what this would do to our economic systems!

Now, I am not suggesting that it's either possible or desirable to implement Jubilee in contemporary culture. Kim Tan observes that even in the days of Jesus the existence of vast urbanised wealth and the extensive Gentile land ownership makes the implementation of the original framework impractical, particularly under the domination of the Roman Empire.

However, the underlying values cut right to the heart of our attitudes to God, possessions, wealth, the land and lifestyle in general. In fact, it could be observed that much of what comes under the guise of contemporary Christianity is living in darkness in these areas, being closer to the ways of Babylon than to the ways of God. Babylon came to symbolise an empire that was anti-God and Christ in its corruption and orientation in later biblical literature (see the book of Revelation).

This flows out of the experiences of Israel in Babylonian exile (see 2 Kings 25:13 and the book of Daniel). I think it's time for some radical rethinking. It's also time for us to ask questions around how deep our faith goes. Maybe it has affected our beliefs and permeated our relationships, but has it really gone to the root of our lives? The Jubilee poses this question.

What's required is not adherence to a list of principles and hard work to implement Jubilee but **faith**. In Leviticus 25:20, God anticipates this question from his Israel:

"You may ask, 'What will we eat in the seventh year if we do not plant or harvest our crops?' I will send you such a blessing in the sixth year that the land will yield enough for three years."

A core requirement for living the Jubilee is a faith-filled confidence in God. Faith that God is good, able and willing to provide what only he can provide to make life work. The lesson here is that no living system, life, worldview, legal system or sociological framework of any kind, no matter how based it is in biblical thinking, works without faith in God and obedience to him.

What God requires is not the implementation of a dry economic system, but the embracing of a life where God himself is at the centre of everything. In this place we realise that all life proceeds from him and that 'fullness of life' is accessed through relationship with him and obedience to his ways. In the words of Jesus in John 10:10:

"The thief comes only to steal and kill and destroy; I have come that they may have life, and have it to the full."

This is only possible as we grow in faith.

Hebrews 11:6 says:

"And without faith it is impossible to please God, because anyone who comes to him must believe that he exists and that he rewards those who earnestly seek him."

In Jubilee we see the closing of the gap between the rich and the poor derived from a mind-blowing, radical and relational economic approach that could only come from God. It's absolutely phenomenal!

However, Israel never implemented it.

Furthermore, if you look in Leviticus 26:23-34, 32-35 and 43, you can see that God's judgment came upon Israel because its people failed to press through. The vision and command of Jubilee was never actualised.

Jeremiah 34: 8-17 indicates that because Israel reneged on the Jubilee agreement and did not free their Hebrew servants, God had brought judgment upon them. I believe that today the Holy Spirit is poised to bless and to release God's goodness in our land but is restricted by the injustice, ignorance, indifference and unrighteous attitudes held by us, his people.

It's not that he is active in judging us vindictively, but that we are reaping the consequences of what we sow or indeed omit to sow. Our blindness and lack of insight, faith and obedience are the limiting factors binding us into a low-level experience of the abundant life we have in Christ, who brings Jubilee to earth.

I realise that so much work is required to fully unpack the Jubilee and contextualise it appropriately. There are some great books out there and I would encourage you to get reading.

But most importantly, why not dream a little, find some co-conspirators and begin to live some of this life in a way that blesses others and brings good news? Imagine what it would be like if some of these values began to influence us? When we read about the New Testament Church you'll see that's exactly what happened to them.

Let's begin to dream. How could some of these values begin to undergird our attitudes to lifestyle, giving and justice? How could some of these values be incorporated within our businesses, portfolios, attitude to loans and materialistic ideals? What tidal waves of liberation and release could be catalysed if we started to think and act differently with some new foundations in place?

Imagine

Imagine businesses, charities, the media, banks, shops and farms beginning to express the heart of this message. Imagine how God's goodness and generosity could break out as people are blessed by the kind of freedom described by the Jubilee.

In quoting Isaiah 61 and by building on Isaiah 58 as seen in Luke 4, Jesus began his ministry with a Jubilee message. In fact, everything that we've looked at so far revolves around Jesus proclaiming the Jubilee.

I want to make it clear, I'm not a Sabbatarian. I believe that if you want to observe the Sabbath, don't worry about Sunday, it's a Saturday! I believe that Jesus was the fulfilment of the Sabbath. When I received Christ and began to enjoy the freedom of salvation, I entered the Sabbath twenty-four seven.

I entered the Sabbath rest, a rest that's in Christ, not in a day of the week. Therefore, religious rules and attitudes around Sunday are not required by Scripture post-Jesus' ministry on earth. Of course, if you are a Messianic Jew (a Jew who believes in Jesus) and you want to observe the Sabbath as a means of identifying with your culture by way of preference or for the purpose of mission then that's perfectly permissible from a biblical perspective.

That's not my calling, neither is this the path for the majority of Christians. However, I believe without doubt that the one-in-seven principle is a good value for the whole of humanity. I'm concerned that Western culture demands competition, immediacy and that trading laws mean that many are without healthy rhythms of rest or family life. This further pressurises the family as a unit, which is at the core of the economy of God as we see it in the Bible.

As family life is eroded, the wellbeing of every human being is downgraded socially, economically and the national 'feel-good factor', which the government currently seems to be interested in, is depressed, unsettled and undermined.

These are concerns shared by many outside of faith-based circles including some within trade unions. This is because, as human beings, we need a rhythm, and the Sabbath dimension teaches that God has set a beautiful order and rhythm in creation. A rhythm of work, rest and play. A relational rhythm. All those things should be elements within our spirituality.

Furthermore, we are not designed to live in an unsustainable manner. Greed promotes indebtedness and injustice, both in those who are subject to debt and in those who make their money from the indebtedness of others. Ultimately, both parties are worse off, even those who become rich financially. We must remember that at times within Old Testament prophesy unbridled riches are seen as a judgement from God because of the corruption to the human soul that often follows.

Some friends of ours required a small amount of capital to take their business to the next level. They run a very successful catering business but had had a business failure in the past. As a result of this past, their high street bank would only lend to them at 18% interest. This would have crippled business growth and made their successful business vulnerable to failure. That same bank would have lent to others with a better credit record at 7.5%.

This is just a small example of how our communities are being crippled by an unjust financial system where the weak are further weakened. This type of scenario makes no sense economically in the long term. As people's progress is halted or hindered, their family and relational life is further stressed with potential health, marital and other issues, which all use up more of society's resources. Our current system could do with an overhaul from top to bottom. However, without God at the centre, would the next system be any more just? I doubt it.

We need to explore what righteous lending looks like and also deal with covetousness, which lures many into the debt trap. That's where the transforming inner work of God's grace comes in. Without this transformation I doubt that many human beings would have the necessary heart and impetus to live according to a radically different approach to life. Personal greed fuels both foolish and irrational borrowing as well as immoral lending. Only a deep personal and spiritual rebirth can shift these issues, and that's right at the core of why Jesus came offering this experience to all.

This message of Jubilee portrays the heart of God, and as the Church, we are called to be a community that embodies the values of Jesus. Dealing with the issues of debt and empowerment, seeing God's Holy Spirit break out, people experiencing salvation, healing, being set free and established relationally and economically in their own right – this is the message of Jubilee.

How on earth do we begin to embrace it?

Slot machine syndrome

I'm not saying that God's economy is like a kind of divine slot machine. "Thou prayeth this and God giveth that." Some people have a naive and misplaced worldview whereby, as we give a pound, God gives back ten pounds. This is a kind of spiritual Ponzi scheme that will ultimately crash to earth when reality dawns.

God blesses us with his goodness in success, failure, darkness and light. He delivers us from the fire of pain and adversity, but also when we are within those fires. We rarely get to choose our options, but nevertheless we have the joy and security of tasting the life and goodness of God in any and every experience. We don't know what's going to happen, but what we do know is that God is good and that he is with us. Serving him, and sowing all we are and have in him, is the way to fulfilment.

The teaching of Jesus encourages us towards faith and experimentation. It provokes the question, "What does it mean for us to live the economy of God in our families, in our churches and from a missions point of view in our communities?"

Because we live in a world where systems have replaced the fear of the Lord. I love Proverbs 9. Its centrepiece is: "The fear of the Lord is the beginning of wisdom" (Proverbs 9:10).

The proverb presents two women. The first, Wisdom, is sitting in the marketplace, setting out her wares. She's saying, "Come to me." At the same time, the second woman, Folly, is also looking for recruits. Those that follow Folly follow corruption and their lives ultimately fall to pieces leading to the "grave", while those who follow Wisdom find life and understanding.

We live in a society where communism crumbled, and those invested in capitalism said, "Well, we always said it was a bad system". As communism rotted from within, its demise caused a temporary feeling of "I told you so" in the West.

Now we're living in a capitalist system that's also rotting from within. We are in this culture and we're going to suffer the backwash. It's time for Christians to anchor themselves in Christ, the wisdom of God, and to stop running after the Folly that's being served up within many areas of our hedonistic culture.

Peace

The good news is that there is a rhythm, an order that God has given us that enables us to live in contentment, regardless of what is happening, because his economy is much bigger than just global finance.

What I like about the Old Testament is that no matter how feckless those that are following God are at times, the favour of the Lord is still upon them, at least for a season until they learn. Even the great Abraham was prone to bouts of cowardly behaviour. Why not take half an hour to read the story in Genesis 20 and meditate on it for a while?

When Abraham and his entourage moved into Abimelech's territory he was concerned for his wellbeing. His wife Sarah was very beautiful and he thought he might be killed so she could be taken by another. So he pretended that Sarah was not his wife, but his sister. Abimelech then took Sarah as his wife until God intervened in a dream, warning him of his impending death because Sarah was a married woman!

Abimelech is quite naturally stunned and confronts Abraham, who confesses that it was his fear that caused him to lie. The result of this was that none of the women in Abimelech's household could conceive.

Nevertheless, because Abimelech feared the Lord and Abraham was God's chosen, Abimelech gave him considerable riches. Despite his fear, when Abraham prayed over Abimelech, God answered his prayer. His household was healed of barrenness and children were conceived once more.

At times, God's loving grace and his commitment to creating a people worthy of his name causes him to work somewhat creatively with our weaknesses. We often think that in success we have been 'right'. More often, it's that God has been faithful to the promise he made us when we gave our lives to Christ and has made the best of our limited capacity. The blessing of the Lord is powerful and literally changes our destiny and the lives of those closest to us. At the same time this blessing overflows to others within our communities as we pray and live 'in Jesus' name', even though we are imperfect.

I love this quote by Marcus Curnow about God's economy.

> *The biblical understanding of economy is grounded in the ancient Hebrew spiritual exercise of keeping Sabbath. It is neither solely material nor spiritual, but extends to encompass all aspects of what it means to produce and consume as a living being. Beyond money, this economy includes elements of time, of energy, of work, of recreation, of relationship with the spiritual, the created order and other people.*

Isn't that beautiful? God has a good order that's revealed in Scripture. He's given us great gifts in creation and one another that will see us through, no matter what.

The biblical story is God's big plan, beginning in the garden and finishing in the city. But the subtext is his blessing, guidance and relationship with his people. Whether they are in slavery, captivity, minority, defeat, chaos, famine, abundance or persecution, God's hand is upon them. Somehow they always come out smelling of roses. Somehow faith delivers them from the fire. Somehow God's hand is upon them and this can be visibly recognised by those around them, even if their blessing is not always interpreted correctly and attributed to God.

We are all impacted by these times of global instability. However, we should be encouraged, like Paul in prison in Philippi, that God's economy transcends all this and is far deeper and wider.

Don't fear the freeze

This realisation fills me with wonder and excitement. I'm challenged by the rhythms of God in nature as there has been a lot of talk about the 'economic freeze'. This produces fear within me; fear about the future.

Surprise, surprise, this makes me think about my fish farm. During a recent winter, Steve and I went back to one of our stock ponds to harvest some fish. We had loaded all our paraphernalia onto the trailer. There was quite an array of equipment. We had one-hundred-metre and forty-metre seine nets, tanks, weighing gear, thermal underwear and, most importantly, dry suits. We left early, in the dark, on a cold January morning. On arrival at the site we were immediately deflated by the sight before our eyes. The lake was frozen, literally frozen solid!

So I looked at Steve, who's a bit of a 'Jim'll Fix It' type, and asked, "What are we going to do?"

He said: "We're going to break the ice in a semi-circle across the entire lake and pull the net underneath it.

"Oh great," I replied, without much enthusiasm. So I put my dry suit on, jumped down on the ice and bounced on top of it. It was solid.

He said: “That doesn’t matter, we’ll get in there and somehow we will break through.”

I looked at the lake and it was so frozen – it looked dead. It was a deep dark blue colour. I just thought, “There’s going to be nothing alive in there”.

Gingerly we entered the freezing water. Fortunately the dry suits enabled us to keep warm, floating and bouncing along the bottom where it wasn’t too deep. We began to push ourselves up onto the ice and smash it with our body weight, pulling the boat with the net behind to enable us to set the net under the ice. As we did this the lake was freezing behind us. It was so thick that my friend, who’s not exactly the brittle type, broke one of his ribs as he threw himself onto the ice to break it. At this stage his language became a little more colourful!

To add to the comedy, some of the shooting set who hunt pheasant on the land came by, looking aghast at us standing in freezing water up to our necks.

“By Jove, you guys are jolly hardcore aren’t you?!” was their observation.

“Either that or completely bonkers,” was my retort.

About halfway round I started to doubt, I started to become fearful. There I was in the middle of the lake, out of my depth, in the freezing water. Despite hanging onto the boat and the safety of the dry suit my confidence was faltering. I also began to think, “This is a complete waste of time, we are going to catch absolutely nothing.”

Eventually we made it to the shore and we pulled the net to the bank from under the ice. Each pull brought the net floats closer and we could see them under the ice. At the same time we had to lift big slabs of ice out of the water to make way for the removal of any fish, which at this stage I thought was a waste of time. My mind was asking the question: *"Will there be any life under this freeze?"*

Suddenly, the net drew close and as the pocket at the back was pulled in we saw what was really happening under the ice. The net was teeming with fish and some really big ones too. We were absolutely amazed and marvelled in the truth that, even under this freeze, there was so much life and activity. The lake and its inhabitants were still thriving, even if their metabolism was moving at a slower rate than in the summer. They were also several pounds bigger than the year before, what a result!

As I returned home I felt God speak to me through this experience. Even though the global economy is frozen, actually there is no freeze in God's economy. There is so much potential life and activity that can be activated if we reject fear and embrace faith in God and his provision. We have unlimited resources in Christ.

The principles and values of Jubilee are dynamic and they summon us as a Church to be God's household. We are called to embody this economy and to proactively embrace faith, reject fear and to invest wholeheartedly together in the ways of God. As we do this we learn how to live abundant life, even in a freeze.

The household of God

If you are a believer in Jesus, I want to welcome you into the household of God, his Church. In the New Testament, the root word for economy is translated as "household" and used as a descriptor for the people of God.

The economy of God consists of his values and frameworks, which are continually introduced and repeated as themes within Scripture. These themes include the Sabbath, community and family. As a church begins to bond more coherently together as a unit, which is more authentically reflective of New Testament norms than defective and obsolete traditions, we begin to ask questions and act accordingly.

How many lawnmowers do you need? How many skills do you need? In the economy of God, when things start to come together, we begin to provide for others and receive God's provision through the giving and receiving of our diverse skills and resources.

Every human being has a need, a need for close family relationships, for friendships with identity and within community. For connection with their tribes and nationalities. That's part of the economy. That's the way God's made us as human beings.

As the Old Testament passages reveal, family is another part of God's economy. God created family and his ideal involves healthy family and relationships. However, Scripture is realistic and pragmatic. We live in a society where family is increasingly being broken down. This means as Christians we need to make it up as we go along a little and allow God's redemptive work to restore families and also create all kinds of creative extended models within our orbit.

These create spaces for the wonders of God's grace to be woven into everyday relationships in a way that's naturally supernatural.

That way we will see people whose lives are broken and fragmented bonded together through the love of Christ.

I believe marriage, instituted in the creation narrative and endorsed by Jesus, is right at the heart of God's economy for male and female relationships, the birth and nurture of healthy and whole children and as a secure anchor point for the building of family and extended family within the context of our communities. I have no space to unpack this here.

I believe the entrepreneurial spirit and living by faith are also part of God's economy. These should lead us to engage with the question: how do we walk by faith when we get paid by our boss or by an institution?

Serving God encourages us to understand that even if we're getting paid from another source, we are primarily called to work for God, acting and working in faith and obedience to him as well us fulfilling our jobs to the best of our abilities, with his help. As we do this, God's Spirit breaks out and his economy is released. We take these values into the marketplace and all kinds of miraculous phenomena occur.

We talked about redemption lift in the last chapter, about how salvation is an economic event in the broadest sense. It affects the whole of life. In the past, sociologists have looked at the Methodist and other revivals and have seen that they often trigger significant times of revival economically. It was John Wesley, after all, who coined the phrase 'social holiness', a holiness that affects the whole of life. We noted the observation of Matthew Parris who observes that a certain type of missionary work is key to the future of Africa.

Personal salvation precedes community transformation. It changes our mindsets, bringing with it a whole new life. People start loving and caring, and they stop abusing others. This changes lives, a change that can eventually be measured in broader economic terms. People are freed to work and create wealth, not merely because they want wealth, but because they're created to work and want to make their contribution. As they remain close to Christ they will then use their newly acquired wealth more wisely and generously by redistributing it in different ways and investing and spending it faithfully.

The Church is called to imbibe these values. We're not here to create middle-class, individualistic feeding stations where people can come in and go out experiencing the life of the Spirit and the word of God without ever being yoked to his purposes and rooted in community.

I believe, as churches, we should aspire to something greater. When we dare to navigate the difficult paths of going deeper we begin to experience the peace and the shalom of the Lord, which covers the whole area of life and relationships. It's his peace and contentment.

1 Timothy 3:15 talks about the church as the household of God. This is the Greek word "economy". As Chinese Christian author and church leader Watchman Nee wonderfully observes:

"God's economy is his household administration to share his life in Christ into his chosen people. That he may have a house, a household which reflects his glory. This household is the church, the body of Christ."

Bring it on! When I became a Christian I thought that church was dead, boring and useless, and then I fell in love with Jesus, and one day I opened the New Testament and read Acts 2:42-47. This changed everything for me.

I fell in love with the New Testament vision of God's church. Here is a community that loved Jesus. They were passionate about God and willing to actually live it out amid their weaknesses and regardless of their circumstances. That's what set me on my journey, a journey that I will remain committed to until my dying breath.

God wants to renew our passion to live and build authentic church life. To realise that church is the community of the King. His Spirit is uniquely upon us, his people, as we gather corporately together. We may be weak, stupid and incompetent in certain areas. But if we can manage to get together, serve Jesus and hang onto one another, making it up as we go along, we might just get there – by God's grace! If we learn to forgive one another, support one another and serve passionately as God's co-workers wherever we are called, maybe we'll taste heaven on earth as we move in and out of each other's lives.

In Ephesians 1:10, Paul hints at this economy, referring to the time in the future when the purposes of God reach their fulfilment. When God's economy reaches its fullness, the new heaven and the new earth will have arrived and the vision of Jubilee will be fully experienced.

In the meantime, in chapter 3:2, Paul talks about his message:

"Surely you have heard about the administration of God's message – the economy of God's grace that was given to me for you."

In verse nine he mentions economy again:

"And to make plain to everyone the economy of this mystery."

God's economy is his arrangement, his order. We are called to love and live the created order, the economy of God. Sometimes we react, "Order? We want messy church!" We want something exciting and spontaneous. Nevertheless, from Paul's angle the good news of the gospel involved "making plain" his intentions, his economy and his administration for the whole of creation.

If you want to know what God's order is like, pick a really clear night and go and stand where there's little ambient lighting, look into the heavens and behold the beautiful array of stars. Some smaller, some bigger. See the planets. See the delicate balance that God has put in place, each one a perfect distance from the other to enable the whole universe to function and for life to be possible on earth. This is God's order and it's truly awesome.

That's why the psalmist cries out: "The law of the Lord is wonderful, it's pure, it's beautiful. The fear of the Lord is tremendous" (Psalm 19:7-11). Because God's order is so glorious and we are called to seek after it. His order in creation, within human relationships and sexuality, within family life, communities and among nations is beautiful. It should be our passion and desire. There's no other order that has existed or will ever exist that could come near it, either in terms of beauty or in terms of functionality.

As the presence of God comes and shakes our lives it's time for us to re-evaluate. God is calling his Church to live up to its name, to become an expression of the manifesto of Jesus. You may think: "Our church is only tiny, we're only twenty or thirty people." You can't do everything, so just pick something. If you aim at nothing, that's what you will hit. If you aim at something the least you will do is miss.

Somebody once said: *"I want to be doing something for God when Jesus comes back, even if it's making mistakes!"*

Same old Saviour, always saving!

In the days when Alan Shearer was centre forward for Newcastle United, the sound from the terraces was always, "Same old Shearer, always scoring".

Well I think we could be singing a slightly adjusted but similar song to God!

A marriage is restored. A child finds security. A father learns how to love his son. His son is able to go back to school because his anxiety has reduced. The son's behaviour spectacularly improves, he can now study because he can now focus. He couldn't study before but now he begins to receive high grades. The next minute he's off to university. People see the outward success but miss that, underneath, it's a work of God.

I never made university, I was too busy vacuously head-banging to metal music and partying. I didn't quite finish my A-levels either. I just head-banged my way through the lot! Somehow in the process I found Jesus. I hadn't really read a book until I came to Christ but I couldn't stop reading afterwards.

I used to work for the Inland Revenue and in my first appraisal my boss said to me: *"Well Roger, you're a square peg in a round hole."*

This was not a great appraisal. Clearly it was not going to be a career for me, but it didn't matter; I had experienced Christ, and as I pursued him I found myself rooted in God, leading friends to Christ, learning about Scripture and starting a church, all in the space of about three years. My whole life attitude was gradually and radically changed. I was able to step out of the dysfunctional mindsets and limited vision I had for my life to embrace the broad vista of the purposes of God. It feels to me like that's when my life really began in earnest. I never looked back and have no plans to begin doing so more than thirty years later.

Conversion changes lives. Building from there is a process of sanctification (being made more like Jesus) because transformation doesn't all happen at once. We have been saved, we are being saved and we will be saved. At times we have to fasten our safety belts as we go through the shaky process of repentance (radical changes in mindset, opinion and direction), letting go of anything that doesn't fit with our new-found faith as quickly as we can in order to at the same time embrace as much as we can of this new life in Christ in as short a time as possible. At least, that was my tactic.

As we cooperate with him, God's economy comes slowly and steadily into our lives and begins to reorder us. We begin to embrace the right priorities and our ambitions are refined and purified. As this happens we begin to experience God's peace in our hearts.

We are then able to begin walking in the Holy Spirit, which also has economic ramifications. There's a lot of talk about orientation in our society, mainly around the issues of sexuality. Well, have you ever asked yourself what the Holy Spirit's orientation is?

Acts 2:42-47 shows that, right at the heart of the coming of the Holy Spirit, there is this orientation towards Jubilee. Acts 2 records the coming of the Holy Spirit; 3,000 people turning to Christ in one day. In response:

> *They devoted themselves to the apostles' teaching and to fellowship, to the breaking of bread and to prayer. Everyone was filled with awe at the many wonders and signs performed by the apostles. All the believers were together and had everything in common. They sold property and possessions to give to anyone who had need. Every day they continued to meet together in the temple courts. They broke bread in their homes and ate together with glad and sincere hearts, praising God and enjoying the favour of all the people. And the Lord added to their number daily those who were being saved.*

That's it, these four or five verses contain everything I've mentioned so far, in a more concise way!

I believe the orientation of the Holy Spirit is towards this kingdom, good news, Jubilee smoothie. God has mixed his calling and vocation and invested it in us his people, releasing us to serve it out in all its diversity.

We are here as the Church to lay out, to implement God's economy, his kingdom on the earth. We know that it can only come through the power of the Holy Spirit, yet God has given us the tools and said, *"Get on with it"*. The kingdom of heaven is forcefully advancing, and forceful men and women lay hold of it (Matthew 11:12).

According to Jesus, the kingdom of heaven is at hand. It is within reach, so all we need to do is reach out, grab hold of it and bring it to earth.

I love that it's about practical everyday life. Often it's about good, faith-filled choices and the careful investment of our hearts, lives and resources. It was Baptist minister George Eldon Ladd who said: *"The basic demand of the kingdom of God is a response of the will."*

I also love that at times it's outrageous and inexplicable. Sometimes the Holy Spirit is way ahead of us and we are called just to join in and run after him as doors open up.

We should be excited by the fact that the kingdom also comes as communities of people live, serve and conspire together. It arrives as we sit down with our friends and we talk economics, giving and financial planning. It comes as we talk about our hopes, fears and dreams and begin to see that in God we can achieve more than we could ever conceive in our own strength.

We begin to adjust our sights more towards God. We work together and pray together to see transformation. We bring his order of life into our lives and that makes the difference. We realise that if we just thrash ourselves into the ground living like others who have no faith our lives will bear limited fruit; however, if we live lives for God then who knows what wonderful things might be accomplished?

POSTCARDS FROM MY FRIENDS · JULIAN & SARAH RICHARDS

Julian and Sarah Richards have been friends of mine for many years. I can remember meeting them before their move to Swansea and we have kept in touch ever since. The story of their journey is immense and could fill a whole book in itself. Their story is a great example of 'essence in action'.

Cornerstone's story

Our experience of the Holy Spirit at work in the community, breaking through barriers of social exclusion, bringing wholeness and healing to broken hearts and bodies, and transforming despair into hope tells a story of the Holy Spirit's interaction in our world today.

After six years in ministry working as evangelists, on church missions, restarts and in church-planting situations, God led me and Sarah to pioneer a church in the north of Swansea. There were nine of us, mainly in our late teens and twenties. On November 5, 1991, we launched our church plant with a bonfire party at our house.

God had led us to buy a big old Victorian house in the north of the city. This purchase was a miracle. However, the house was in a poor state, with no heating or hot water, and as church planters we had very little income. Amazingly, within a month of moving in, the house came to the top of the list for a council grant and got totally refurbished inside and out.

The house became properly habitable and was used as a base for all our church meetings and activities. Although we were all young and poor, and for us personally the first seven years or so were very hard, we saw incredible provision from God during this season. This built in us faith and determination, and however small or poor we were, our little church plant began to get on with serving our community.

We started working with schools and other community groups, running events and special meetings. The local area contained a mixture of private housing alongside large council estates, where the social and economic need was great. People living in these areas were experiencing the effects of poverty and high unemployment, poor literacy, crime and teenage pregnancy. In working-aged adults, 53% had no qualifications at all, 60% of homes had no car and just under half the homes relied on benefits to make ends meet. Our car was stolen regularly and our house and garden were frequently burgled (a total of sixteen times in seven years). We started to be challenged about how to meet the needs of the community and to reach them with the gospel in such challenging circumstances.

The church grew to thirty in a couple of months. On Sundays we started meeting in a community centre, a breezeblock building with no windows; it was rather bleak. Meetings here were certainly 'interesting', with fights breaking out as I was preaching and impromptu 'mattress bonfires' in the car park after youth events. One local visitor commented that our meetings were rougher than "a night at Dora's Disco". It was not unusual to find your tax disc or car parts missing when you came back to the car park.

We held concerts and competition events in the schools, but after one of these competitions, the kid who won was beaten up outside. We realised that our community work had to be more strategic and suited to the immediate needs we were witnessing. We began a whole new range of community projects centred on education. We also felt we needed a centre of our own to be able to serve the community in a new strategic way.

One day I drove past our Post Office sorting office and saw it was for sale. I thought, "This would be a great place for a church". Sarah and I looked around the premises with the estate agent and felt God wanted us to buy it. It was terribly vandalised but otherwise perfect. The asking price was £35,000. Considering the economic state of the area and the size and means of the congregation, this was very steep.

The church took a deeply sacrificial offering and raised £8,000 for a mortgage deposit – an astoundingly generous amount. Yet the mortgage company was concerned by the limited amount of regular income so, as a church, we all decided to start giving more than 10% of our incomes on a regular basis. The building was ours!

God stirred our vision with regard to using the building for community projects: an alternative curriculum for disaffected youth, toddler groups, counselling services and health classes. Yet the practicalities of transforming these ideas into reality seemed incredible. The building was ours but it was initially totally unusable without extensive refurbishment. It sat there for another two years empty. I said to God: "You've called us to work in this community and have given us a building and a vision, yet we don't have the resources, people or money to bring this to fruition." I heard the Holy Spirit assure me, "As you need it, I will provide it." We were starting to feel frustrated with the lack of progress then three things happened in answer to that prayer.

First, we really needed an entrepreneurial administrator to secure grants for the refurbishment required to start the projects we wanted to run. Through an unusual series of events, an old friend with these skills got in touch out of the blue and moved to us for a season to start fundraising and to secure some early grants. This was the first answer.

Second, the Holy Spirit nudged me to "ask the church to give again", as we had grown since the initial purchase. I was very reluctant, as the church had given so sacrificially already out of the little they had. But when I suggested it the response was simply staggering – it was met with a round of spontaneous applause! We raised £15,000. Within fourteen days this was matched by a grant of £15,000 from Tearfund for UK community work. Now we were off to a start with our finances, but our centre needed drastic attention.

Our third answer to prayer came next. After preaching at a local church, a Christian businessman came up to me and asked to see our building. As we showed him around he explained that his business was in renovating and refurbishing buildings. We only had £30,000 but he generously completed the entire refurbishment, partly at his own expense. We were quite overwhelmed by this generous provision. Our work all over the community now had a base for staff and projects.

Cornerstone Church Centre and Cornerstone Community Project launched publicly in January 1998. Jeff Lucas cut the ribbon and opened our centre, and the opening was full of local people, teachers, counsellors and families who had supported the planting process and come to our events and projects over the years.

Due to the growth of the church and success of the community work, we ran out of space within one year. Through a European grant, we were able to build a £100,000 extension. God had provided a centre for the church, and we were then able to develop our vision for becoming a vital part of our community and seeing people's lives transformed by God's love and power.

Over the years we have run a number of projects, on and off site. It has been amazing to see people's lives touched both by the power of the healing community of God's people, and also the social transformation brought about by the projects. We researched the needs of the community and matched those needs wherever we had the skills or resources. People in the church who were passionate for an issue brought ideas for projects and ran them with enthusiasm.

One of our projects, The Gap, was birthed out of a whisper from the Holy Spirit. I was out walking around the local reservoir, concerned for the young people in our area dropping out of school. Truancy was a huge problem, and by the age of fourteen a large percentage of young people were drifting from school into unemployment and adding to the economic inactivity in our area. Many became involved in crime and drug activity.

God gave me the picture of a kind of 'learning through leisure' concept. This seed idea became The Gap. The Gap began in January 1998 and ran until 2010, touching two thousand young people in the city. Sarah became the project director with an enthusiastic team of four from the church giving up jobs to become a part of this new venture. The project was designed to fill the gap between school and work for fifteen- and sixteen-year-olds.

We pioneered an alternative type of curriculum based on indoor/outdoor learning. As funds came in we trained our team members to become outdoor pursuits instructors and youth tutors. We became an accredited outdoor activity provider and became an accredited learning centre. Funding equipped us with wetsuits and surfboards, kayaks, and all kinds of outdoor equipment and our own Gap mini bus.

Challenged, deprived and marginalised young people disaffected with school would come on the course for nine months and gain qualifications and skills that allowed them to progress to training or employment. The success of the young people in terms of responding to the course and changing their lives was beyond our expectations. Young people who had been truanting became 100% attendees. Young people who were failing gained qualifications. They developed the ability to communicate, work with others and acquired the skills necessary to hold down a job. We made many relationships in the community.

In the education world, news got out fast and The Gap team contributed to conferences and seminars across the UK on youth disaffection. Sarah spoke alongside a government inspector for education to senior educationalists and investors about the role of the church in changing communities. The Gap featured in Welsh Assembly consultation documents and research into educational methods. It contributed to changing the future face of education in Wales by sharing good practice and its keys to success.

The success of the project exceeded our expectations as young people progressed to the workplace across our community. The crime rate declined considerably. The Gap ran on funding from the generosity of grant-giving trusts, and although securing funding was hard work, the success statistics for working with challenged young people in such a deprived area began to attract funding for a project that genuinely worked.

The Gap won the Youth Work in Wales Excellence Award and the Lord Mayor's Community Regeneration Award for outstanding contribution to community regeneration in the city and county of Swansea two years running. Sarah and The Gap team became well respected in the field and were invited to speak at major events in London, Birmingham and Cardiff, exploring education for disaffected young people with educationalists and politicians.

The knock-on effect for education policy has been amazing. The Welsh Assembly acknowledged the achievement of The Gap, which has helped to pioneer and shape the delivery of an alternative curriculum in Wales. This means that youngsters gain from the personalised approach to meeting their needs, investing in them the life skills they need to build their own futures.

From the initial prompting of the Holy Spirit to engage young people in outward bound activities and educate them in skills and gain qualifications, when we lacked resources, skills and people, to the staggering results of The Gap, we have witnessed God breaking into and transforming the lives of individuals for good.

Another local issue was the high teenage pregnancy rate. Out of the first pilot group of fifteen girls who attended The Gap, five were pregnant by the end of the course. We began to teach on pregnancy issues and the next year none of the girls who came to The Gap fell pregnant. This led to the creation of a new project called Soulmates.

Soulmates was a creative and interactive lesson-based project going into schools to teach classes about sexual health, relationship skills and parenting preparation. This contributed to Swansea seeing the highest drop in teenage pregnancy in the UK. As a result, the church was invited to sit on two council committees for youth and sexual health for the city and county of Swansea.

Around this time we were running a pre-school toddler group, a homework club, The Gap, Soulmates, adult education classes, Picture This (digital photography classes), computer classes, a kid's football club and a community counselling service. Alongside these projects we were running a year-round programme of evangelism, social events, special guest meetings and Alpha.

The success of the community projects resulted in an invitation for me to become chaplain to the mayor. This positioned me in dialogue with the city cabinet, giving the church a voice of greater influence and allowing a more collaborative approach to serving the city. The Holy Spirit's prompting for community social action has therefore not only transformed individual lives but has also influenced policy and practice across the city.

As we developed the community projects, it became clear that the church as a whole lacked an umbrella organisation to represent its community work to government. So Cornerstone, together with Tearfund, CARE and the Evangelical Alliance set up Gweini (which means "Serve"), a body designed to represent the Christian voluntary sector to the Welsh Assembly and local government.

Before the founding of this body, churches were often refused funding because they were faith-based organisations. However, Gweini succeeded in raising the perception of the church in the government's eyes, and now the church's community contribution is encouraged, welcomed and funded.

Gweini initiated Wales's first faith audit, a survey to evaluate the contribution of faith organisations to their communities in Wales, part-funded by the Welsh Assembly and the New Ideas Fund. The survey revealed that churches contribute £100 million of economic benefit to their communities every year. Every week, forty thousand church volunteers give eighty thousand hours for the benefit of their local communities. The church is busy and active right across Wales.

Approaching our twentieth anniversary as a church, Cornerstone continues to be devoted to making the message of Jesus accessible through being a mission-focused community. Combining social care in the community alongside our church evangelism has created a network of varied access points for local people. It has built bridges and widened our reach in the community.

The reputation we've built in the community makes it easy to invite people to church meetings and to church social events. Sunday mornings are designed to be accessible, understandable and enjoyable for the 'unchurched' as well as for the congregation so that the message of Jesus is easily heard. We seek to build authentic friendships by holding many informal social events throughout the year, such as surfing, cinema nights, pub quizzes, curry nights and parties. Cornerstone aims to be a church for the unchurched, to integrate the good news of Jesus with serving the community.

In our experience, a key element in helping people in our community find faith has been supernatural encounters with God, particularly his healing. One lady from the local area was coming along to Picture This. As she walked past our centre one Sunday morning, she heard the singing and decided to come in. She suffered from terribly painful arthritis in one arm and hand, which was very swollen and bent out of shape. She wore a plastic support to spread her hand out so that it wouldn't seize up.

We prayed for her that morning and immediately the pain disappeared. She came back the following week, pain-free but her arm was still swollen. After prayer the swelling disappeared and she threw the plastic support away. She was delighted to be able to cook once again. She began to come to church regularly and joined our Alpha course.

One Sunday she arrived home and put the TV on to find it blaring out. At first she thought the TV was faulty, then realised she had been healed of deafness. She had been deaf in one ear since she was a young girl, so she threw her hearing aid away as well! Following the Alpha course she found faith, got baptised and has been a part of our church family ever since.

On another occasion, a lady was encouraged by her GP to attend our counselling project. A car crash had left her in significant pain and she had sunk into depression. The counselling helped her cope with her depression and we offered to pray with her for physical healing as well. She agreed and immediately the pain left her. As she left the centre, she said, "I feel like I'm walking on air!" Now she was free of both depression and the pain that caused it. Many local people have since experienced God's healing in many everyday situations.

John was a trucker, the husband of one of the church members, and he experienced another great encounter with God's healing power. John's wife had said, "It'll take a miracle for John to become a Christian."

John's son tragically died very unexpectedly and after the funeral at Cornerstone, he was so touched by God that he gave his life to Jesus there and then. He had suffered terribly with a bad back for some years after a nasty accident with a fork lift truck. It would take him twenty minutes to get out of bed or up from a chair. He was in constant pain and wore a weightlifter's leather belt around his torso for support. After receiving prayer in the church car park, he was completely healed. At his baptism he held up the leather belt he no longer needs to wear because his back is healed and we showed a film interview featuring John doing press-ups and jumping over a row of chairs at almost sixty years of age!

Healing stories such as these have given the church members confidence to pray for friends and family members who are sick. We have numerous stories of God's healing in these situations. Some have come to know God as a result, others have just remained grateful. But we know that everyone has had the touch of the kingdom of God and experienced the power of the Holy Spirit.

From Cornerstone's early days with its nine young ambitious founders and £35 in the offering, we have witnessed God's work and provision in a socially deprived area through projects and healing. We have seen lives transformed, with unemployable and anti-social youths in employment all over the city.

We have a lower crime rate and teenage pregnancy has been reduced. There is now funding for church projects across the city. We have been able to contribute to educational policy for our city and nation. We have interacted with local and national government because of the success of practical projects intervening in areas of poverty and deprivation. People are walking around the city free from pain. God has touched people all over the city by the people in the church community– all through the power and equipping of the Holy Spirit. We have now outgrown our current building and are looking for new premises to continue this faith adventure and journey with God.

The challenge for us today is where will the Holy Spirit lead us next? What is the next venture and initiative the Holy Spirit has in store for us? Wherever and whatever, we know he will, as always, provide.